"Dr. Stanley H. Block helps people see their mind as never before by helping t
system and then guiding them through simple mapping exercises to teach
rests their I-System so that they can unblock their potential to deal with their

    —Shirley MacLaine, actress and author of *Out on a Leash* and *The Camino*

"Transform your life in a matter of ten days. I did."

    —Christiane Northrup, MD, author of *Women's Bodies, Women's Wisdom*

"Mind-body bridging is a new body-mind language that allows people to reconnect with their ability to
function effectively. Since I have directly witnessed the power and efficacy of Stan's work, I am very ready
to state that the approach of mapping and bridging can be an adjunct to spiritual practice or it can stand
on its own."

    —Charlotte Joko Beck, bestselling author of *Everyday Zen*

"Dr. Block's bridging methods have given me new ways to help pitchers deal with adversity and compete
in the major leagues."

    —Rafael Chaves of the New York Yankee Organization, former pitching coach for Seattle Mariners

"This mind-body medicine-based workbook guides readers back to their inner reservoir of self-empower-
ment by showing them how to override a learned stress response and faulty brain network and regain access
to their natural executive functioning. The mind-body mapping exercises outlined within teach readers
how to reduce stress and develop a set of personalized, powerful, crisis-management tools. Moreover, since
these exercises are quick and easy to do, they'll become a welcome staple of your lifelong health regimen.
But don't be fooled by their simplicity. I've witnessed their powerful impact personally and in my work
with cancer patients and their caregivers."

    —Michelle Rodoletz, PhD, assistant professor in the department of psychiatry, Fox Chase
        Cancer Center, Philadelphia, PA, and director of the Continuing Education Program for
        HealthForumOnline (www.healthforumonline.com)

MIND-BODY WORKBOOK

for stress

Effective Tools for Lifelong Stress Reduction & Crisis Management

STANLEY H. BLOCK, MD
& CAROLYN BRYANT BLOCK
with ANDREA A. PETERS

NEW HARBINGER PUBLICATIONS, INC.

Distributed in Canada by Raincoast Books

Copyright © 2012 by Stanley H. Block & Carolyn Bryant Block
New Harbinger Publications, Inc.
5674 Shattuck Avenue
Oakland, CA 94609
www.newharbinger.com

All Rights Reserved

Acquired by Jess O'Brien; Cover design by Amy Shoup; Edited by Rosalie Wieder

---

Library of Congress Cataloging-in-Publication Data

Block, Stanley H.
  Mind-body workbook for stress : effective tools for lifelong stress reduction and crisis management / Stanley H. Block, Carolyn Bryant Block, and Andrea A. Peters.
     p. cm.
  Includes bibliographical references.
  ISBN 978-1-60882-636-0 (pbk. : alk. paper) -- ISBN 978-1-60882-637-7 (pdf e-book) -- ISBN 978-1-60882-638-4 (epub) 1. Self-esteem. 2. Stress tolerance (Psychology) 3. Stress (Psychology) I. Block, Carolyn Bryant. II. Peters, Andrea A. III. Title.
  RC489.S43B56 2012
  155.9'042--dc23
                        2012027986

Printed in the United States of America

12 11 10   10 9 8 7 6 5 4 3 2 1   First printing

CONTENTS

ACKNOWLEDGMENTS

Our teaching about stress is primarily influenced by the effective way individuals suffering from stress have shared with us how they utilized Mind-Body Bridging to liberate themselves from the restrictions of the I-System. Although we have not specifically referenced other workers in the stress reduction field, we appreciate their pioneering work. The clinicians from around the world using, developing and refining Mind-Body Bridging have our gratitude and thanks. Deserving of specific mention are the members of the International Mind-Body Bridging Certification Committee: Don Glover, Rich Landward, Theresa McCormick, Andrea Phillips, Isaac Phillips, and Kevin Webb. The research efforts of Yoshi Nakamura, David Lipschitz, and Derrik Tollefson, to establish a firm evidence basis for Mind-Body Bridging is much appreciated. Carol Ann Kent, the MBB coordinator has ably assisted in the preparation of this workbook. The direction from the editors of New Harbinger Publishing was most helpful.

INTRODUCTION

Stress impairs our sleep, damages our health, and prevents us from taking care of ourselves and our responsibilities. Stress drives us to overwork, overeat, drink too much, and take excessive amounts of tranquilizers, pain medications, and sedatives. Our relationships deteriorate, our bodies age prematurely, and we lose brain cells at an accelerated rate. Yes, it's true: stress can shrink your brain. Researchers have found that healthy adults aged eighteen to forty-eight who are subject to significant stressors have decreased brain volume (Ansell et al. 2012).

STRESSORS, STRESS, AND STRESS SYMPTOMS

Physical, social, or psychological stressors are demands that overload us. Stress is the mind's and body's signal that a stressor has drained our physical and emotional resources. Stress may manifest itself as anxiety, fears, worry, depression, irritability, anger, lethargy, muscular tension, assorted aches and pains, overworking, hypertension, overeating, indigestion, diarrhea, constipation, insomnia, poor decision making, and alcohol or drug abuse. Stress negatively affects the quality of your life and prevents you from facing situations with a ready and relaxed mind and body.

CONVERTING STRESS INTO SELF-POWER

Self-power is your innate ability to deal effectively with the stressors in your life without stress overload. Converting stress into self-power isn't medieval alchemy; it's twenty-first-century neuroscience. Our self-power is regulated by a brain network researchers refer to as the *executive functioning network*. It's the powerhouse of our life because it orchestrates moment by moment how we see the world, think, make decisions, and act. When the executive functioning network is disrupted, we are powerless to deal with stress. This stress becomes embedded in our minds and bodies as *distress*.

Recent brain research (Boly, Phillips, Balreau, et al. 2008), along with over a decade of clinical experience by physicians, psychologists, social workers, and researchers (Block and Block 2007; Tollefson et al. 2009; Nakamura et al. 2011; Nakamura et al. forthcoming), shows that it is not the stressors in our life that make us stressed out. It's a brain network that clinical researchers call the *default-mode network*. The default-mode network, or the *Identity System* (*I-System*) as we call it (Block, Ho, and Nakamura 2009), is overactive when we have exaggerated thoughts about ourselves and our experiences. When the I-System is activated our awareness contracts and we have a harder time responding to situations as they come up. Researchers have found that when the I-System is active, the executive functioning network is inactive (Boly, Phillips, Tshibanda, et al. 2008). Only one network can be in the driver's seat at a time (Weissman et al. 2006).

Mind-body bridging, a branch of mind-body medicine, has developed easy-to-apply tools to control your I-System and put the executive functioning network in the driver's seat. Rather than teaching you how to manage your stressors, reduce stress, or relax, this book focuses on how to make that quantum shift from an active to inactive I-System. When your I-System is resting, your self-power is fully functional, and you can immediately defuse stressful situations in your everyday life. Mind-body bridging not only subjectively reduces stress, it has been shown to objectively reduce a stress hormone, alpha-amylase (Lipschitz et al. forthcoming).

MIND-BODY LANGUAGE

Your mind and body do not operate independently of each other; they are an inseparable whole (the *mind-body*). We introduce you to a clinically validated mind-body language that allows you to know, communicate with, and manage your mind and body as never before. This easy-to-understand language frames your mind-body states in terms of an active or inactive I-System, giving you the power to quickly start reducing your stress and reaching your goals.

There are times when life is overwhelming. Your head is full of urgent and pressing "to-do's," your body is full of stressful tension, and you can't see the light at the end of the tunnel. This state of mind and body is the *powerless self*. The powerless self is not simply a mental state; it also affects every cell of your body. It's caused by an overactive I-System, not the stressors in your life.

This workbook is based on the fact that your mind-body (mind and body as a unified whole) knows perfectly well how to deal effectively and efficiently with the stressors in your life without stress overload. When you use the stress reduction and power building tools in this book, you will automatically come to a state of natural harmony and balance in your life. In this mind-body state, your powerful self is functioning in the executive mode and stress is converted into self-power. Each chapter introduces the new mind-body language utilized in that chapter.

HOW TO USE THIS BOOK

This workbook has a very simple, powerful, and easy-to-use structure. Mind-body principles are stated at the beginning of each chapter. You then validate them for yourself through quick, guided, experiential exercises that give you a unique understanding of your mind and body as a whole. At the end of each chapter the stress reduction and power building tools introduced in that chapter are listed so you can integrate them into your everyday life. Each chapter serves as a building block for the next one, so it's important to do the exercises and read each chapter in sequence. As you move through the chapters, your repertoire of stress reduction and power building tools continues to grow, becoming a resource for any situation in your life.

You will find an MBB (mind-body bridging) Self-Power Indicator at the beginning, middle, and end of the book, so you can measure your self-power as it grows. At the end of each chapter there is an MBB Evaluation Scale that lets you know how well you're implementing and integrating the tools you are learning into your everyday life. Building new habits takes time, but once your tools become habits, you will be able to manage any crisis.

CHAPTER 1

TAP INTO YOUR SELF-POWER TO CONTROL STRESS

Principle: The overactive I-System is responsible for stress overload and impaired self-power.

Principle: When the I-System is resting, you have access to your innate power and wisdom and can handle any stressful situation.

Mind-Body Language:

I-System: Everyone has an I-System, and it's either active or resting. You know the I-System is active when your mind is cluttered with spinning thoughts, your body is tense, your awareness contracts, and your mental and physical functioning is impaired. It's called the I-System because it prompts you to falsely identify with your spinning thoughts and physical distress.

Powerful self: How you think, feel, see the world, and act when your I-System is resting. Your mind and body operate harmoniously as a unit and stressors are handled smoothly and efficiently.

Mind-body bridging: When you use the stress reduction and power building tools in this workbook, the mind and body are unified. A bridge is formed from a stressful state with an overactive I-System to a powerful self, functioning in the executive mode.

YOUR REACTION TO STRESS

1. Let's get started so you can personally experience these principles. Think of a current stressful situation. Write it in the oval below. It may be helpful to look at the example map on the following page. Next, take a couple of minutes to scatter whatever thoughts come to mind about the situation around the oval. Be as specific as you can. Work quickly, without self-editing.

STRESSFUL SITUATION

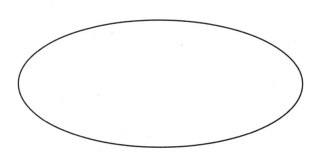

A. Is your mind clear or cluttered with thoughts?

_____

B. Is your body tense or relaxed? List where and how your body is tense:

_____

C. With your mind and body in this condition, how do you act?

_____

You probably think that the stressful situation is what's creating your inner stress, which you see on your map. It's not! You have just experienced your overactive I-System. Your I-System takes an external, stressful situation, creates mind clutter and body tension, and impairs your ability to act. The map you will create in the next part of this exercise will allow you to see what is causing your stress and will teach you the critical first step in converting your inner stress into self-power.

SAMPLE MAP: STRESSFUL SITUATION

We will lose our house

I have too many bills

I have to keep my job

I DON'T HAVE ENOUGH MONEY

My family spends too much

I can't find a good job

I'll never be able to retire

I'm overwhelmed

A. Is your mind clear or cluttered with thoughts?

My mind is cluttered with thoughts about not having enough money

B. Is your body tense or relaxed? List where and how your body is tense:

My shoulders tight, band around my head, stomachache, really tense all over

C. With your mind and body in this condition, how do you act?

Irritable, angry, feel trapped, unable to know what to do

2. The next part of this exercise can change your life forever, because it shows you how to get your I-System to rest. For this important map, it's helpful to be in a room without distractions such as people talking, TV, or distracting electronic devices. Write that same stressful situation (the one you wrote down in the first map) in the below oval. Before you continue, seat yourself comfortably, listen to any background sounds, experience your body's pressure on your seat, feel your feet on the floor, and feel the pen in your hand. Take your time. If you have thoughts, gently return to listening to background sounds and tuning in to your senses. Once you feel settled, start writing whatever comes to mind about the situation. Watch the ink go onto the paper, keep feeling the pen in your hand, and listen to any background sounds. Write for a couple of minutes.

STRESSFUL SITUATION

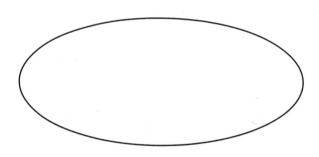

A. Is your mind clear or cluttered with thoughts?

_____

B. Is your body tense or relaxed?

_____

C. How is this map different from the first one you made?

_____

D. Do you have less stress? Yes _____ No _____

E. If you could live your life with your mind-body in this state, do you think you would feel less stress and experience your self-power? Yes _____ No _____

The exercise you just did is a mind-body stress reduction and power building tool called *mind-body mapping*. These two-part mind-body maps are short written exercises that take no longer than a few minutes. Mapping provides a snapshot of your stress level and a gateway to your self-power.

Take a look at the differences between your two completed maps. Your first map shows your stressed-out I-System in action. In the second map, you experienced what it's like to have a resting I-System. You experience that when you literally come to your senses by focusing on your body sensations and the sounds around you, the I-System quiets, and your stress is reduced. Just as your body has the ability to convert the stress imposed on muscles in resistance training to muscle development and power, your mind has the natural ability to convert stressors into the mind-body development of self-power. Mind-body bridging uses the mind and the body to move you from your stressed-out self to your naturally powerful self functioning in the executive mode. Remember, your powerful self is how you think, feel, see the world, and act when your I-System is resting.

When you did your first map, you were full of stress and didn't have enough room left to experience your abundant self-power. When you quiet your I-System as you did in the second map, you are automatically in a more settled state and your ability to handle stress grows (as shown in figure 1.1). Note that the magnitude of the stressful situation hasn't changed. People suffering from stress come to believe that they are a small vessel, filled with stress. No matter how successful you are, when you're stressed, you're using only a small fraction of your self-power. Simply by quieting your I-System, you become an expanded vessel. Your self-power space and problem-solving space expand with mind-body bridging so your natural powerful state resumes. This analogy of having a bigger self-power space is *exactly* how mind-body bridging works. Self-power is the ability to deal with your responsibilities efficiently and effectively, without stress overload. Your ability to handle stress and utilize executive functioning develops on its own. Keep in mind that you don't have to force yourself to achieve self-power—it will develop naturally. Self-power is your birthright.

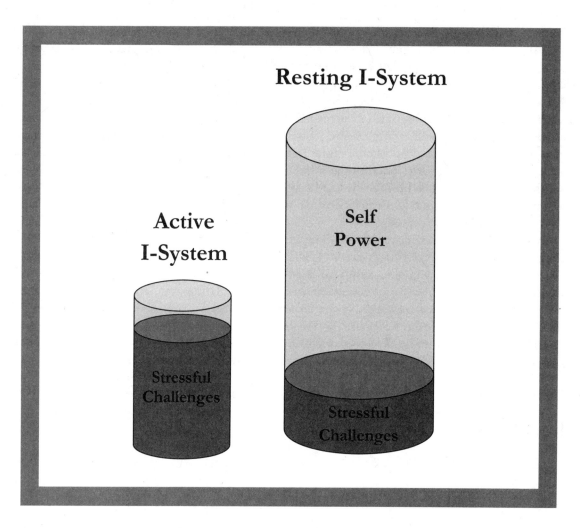

Figure 1.1: Which Vessel Are You In?

When you feel stressed out, you see yourself as a small vessel. You have falsely come to believe that the vessel filled with stress (the darkly shaded area) is all you are. No matter how successful you are, you're still only accessing a fraction of your self-power (the lightly shaded area). It's the overactive I-System that keeps you stuck.

You automatically expand into a bigger vessel when the I-System is resting. The stressful challenges haven't changed, but the capacity of the vessel has. The lightly shaded area in the larger vessel (representing your self-power) expands as you quiet your I-System.

MBB SELF-POWER INDICATOR

Date: _____

It's time to fill out your first MBB Self-Power Indicator. This scale is repeated at intervals throughout the workbook so you can objectively note your progress and systematically keep track of your life-changing experiences.

Think back over the past week while completing the below chart.

Circle the number under your answer.	Not at all	Several days	More than half the days	Nearly every day
1. I've had positive interest and pleasure in my activities.	0	1	3	5
2. I've felt optimistic, excited, and hopeful.	0	1	3	5
3. I've slept well and woken up feeling refreshed.	0	1	3	5
4. I've had lots of energy.	0	1	3	5
5. I've been able to focus on tasks and use self-discipline.	0	1	3	5
6. I've stayed healthy, eaten well, exercised, and had fun.	0	1	3	5
7. I've felt good about my relationships with my family and friends.	0	1	3	5
8. I've been satisfied with my accomplishments at home, work, or school.	0	1	3	5
9. I've been comfortable with my financial situation.	0	1	3	5
10. I've felt good about the spiritual base of my life.	0	1	3	5
11. I've been satisfied with the direction of my life.	0	1	3	5
12. I've felt fulfilled, with a sense of well-being and peace of mind.	0	1	3	5

Score Key: Column Total   ____ ____ ____ ____

0-15 . . . . .Poor Self-Power

16-30 . . . . Fair Self-Power   Total Score _____

31-45 . . . . .Good Self-Power

46 and above . . . . Excellent Self-Power

STRESS REDUCTION AND POWER BUILDING TOOLS

Remember when you did the mapping exercise? When you did the first map you explored a stressful situation. The second map allowed you to explore that same situation with a calmer body and clearer mind. Maybe this state lasted for a while, or maybe it was brief. When making your second map, what pulled you away from hearing the background sounds, feeling the pen, and seeing the ink go onto the paper? Yes, it was your thoughts. The I-System spins your thoughts, makes your body tense, and closes you off from your senses. It converts stressful situations into inner distress and powerlessness. Thought labeling and bridging awareness practices are the tools you will learn in this chapter to help you prevent stress buildup.

THOUGHT LABELING

Your mind naturally makes thoughts (natural thoughts), both positive and negative. You will never get rid of your negative thoughts. In fact, trying to get rid of them doesn't work because when you push them away, you give them energy.

When stressful thoughts come up, it helps to label them using a stress reduction and power building tool called *thought labeling*. Thought labeling lets you see that a thought is *just a thought*. This prevents the I-System from taking a thought, spinning a story from it, crossing the mind-body connection, and creating body tension. Once this happens, the thought is no longer just a thought but a state of mind-body distress.

Let's see how thought labeling works. Think of a stressful situation that creates body tension—for example, *I have too many bills*. When a tension-filled thought pops into your mind, say to yourself, *I'm having the thought "I have too many bills."* Some people even continue with *So, what else is new?* This allows you to learn how you can stop your I-System from capturing your thoughts, taking you away from what you are currently doing.

Ana's boss, an obsessive micromanager, was constantly reminding her how to do her job. The thought *He doesn't trust me* was followed by *He's driving me crazy. Why is he like that? He'll never change.* She began having shoulder tension, neck pain, and headaches. Feeling powerless and stressed about her job, she even considering quitting. After learning how to use mind-body bridging, she developed her stress reduction and power building tools. She recognized that it was her I-System, and not her boss's micromanagement, that was causing her stress. She now labels her thought *He doesn't trust me* as *just a thought,* listens to the background sounds, and continues with the task at hand. As her I-System calmed, her stress decreased, and her physical symptoms subsided. She now feels better when talking to her boss, even though his management style hasn't changed.

Use thought labeling to reduce stress and build self-power. During your day, whenever a thought pulls you away from what you are doing, label that thought and return your awareness to your activity. For example, when you're in the shower and the thought *I'll never get through the day* pops into your mind, say to yourself, *I am having the thought "I'll never get through the day,"* return to your showering, sense the water on your body, and hear the sounds of the shower.

BRIDGING AWARENESS PRACTICES

When the I-System is active, it closes off your senses until all you are aware of is your stress. It's like putting your hands over your ears to block out sounds. The I-System not only keeps you from hearing the ever-present background sounds but also keeps you from experiencing your ever-present self-power. When you use your senses, your I-System quiets, letting you deal with your stressors with a calm, ready mind and a relaxed body.

Bridging awareness practices use your senses to build a bridge from a life filled with stress (the I-System's powerless self) to living life at its best (executive functioning's powerful self). Building this bridge is easier than you think.

Lee was totally committed to his golf game and played frequently in tournaments. Yet it seemed that the harder he tried, the more lessons he had, and the better clubs he bought, the more poorly he played. He was about ready to give up on golf. His friend, who was board certified in mind-body bridging, told him, "I can improve your game in one afternoon." Lee laughed at him but two weeks later took him up on the offer. After Lee learned about bridging awareness practices and mapping, they were off to the driving range. When Lee tried to hit the ball "just right" on each of ten drives, only one was just right. Then he was instructed to use his newly learned bridging awareness tools to feel the club, sense the warm air on his face, hear the hum of the traffic in the background, and simply see the ball. Nine of his next ten drives were excellent. A month later the two men crossed paths. Lee shared the news that his handicap had dropped dramatically—by six strokes—and he was playing his best golf ever. Whenever he was asked, "How well did you play today?" Lee said, "It doesn't matter. I now enjoy playing."

AWARENESS OF BACKGROUND SOUNDS

A fifty-year-old grandfather with a strong mind-body bridging practice detected a lump on his four-year-old grandson's body. At the ER, the diagnosis was leukemia. Rather than retreating into a numb, stressed-out state, the grandfather listened to the sounds in the hospital, felt his feet on the tile floor, became settled, and was able to comfort his family, helping them make decisions about appropriate care.

Your environment is full of sounds. During the day, pause and listen to any background sounds, like the white noise of the heating or air-conditioning system, the wind blowing, traffic sounds, or the hum of the refrigerator or computer. If your thoughts start to spin, gently return your awareness to what you were doing. See what happens to your mind and body when you focus on background sounds.

A young mother of a two-month-old infant became anxious and distraught if her baby cried for more than ten minutes. She would pick the baby up, but when he was put back into the crib, the crying would start again. Using her stress reduction and power building tools she began experiencing the crying in a different way; it became something she could use as a bridging awareness practice (awareness of sounds). With a resting I-System, she relaxed and was able to mother her child. She reported that the baby was now sleeping fine.

AWARENESS OF WHAT YOU ARE TOUCHING

We all touch hundreds of things every day. Were you aware of how it felt under your fingertips today when you touched your shoes, socks, shirt, keys, fork, watch, paper, or computer? Were you aware of your senses when you touched your child or a close friend? Did you sense the warmth of the coffee cup or the coldness of the water bottle in your hand? Chances are you didn't. Your I-System has numbed your body, detaching you from your senses. Tuning in to your sense of touch is another bridging awareness practice that quiets your I-System.

Be aware of what the sensations are like under your fingertips as you touch things like glasses, phones, pens, keys, computers, and other objects. Are they smooth or rough, cold or warm, pleasant or unpleasant? When washing your hands or showering, feel the water as it touches your skin. Sense what it's like to touch others or be touched. This may take some effort, because the I-System dulls your senses. A young, highly stressed student told us that simply sensing his thumb rubbing against his finger calmed him down enough to stop him from getting into unnecessary arguments with his teachers and classmates.

Note what you touch and the sensations you feel during the day. Do you feel more settled when you are aware of what you are touching? Keep practicing!

AWARENESS OF COLORS, FACIAL FEATURES, AND SHAPES

The I-System grasps at certain images while rejecting others. This prevents you from "seeing the whole picture." When you use one or more of your senses, the I-System calms down, your awareness expands, and you actually *see* what's out there. When you look at a sunset or even a speck of dust on the floor, does your busy head let you see its colors, shapes, and uniqueness? Probably not for long. Take a look at your next meal. When your food is in front of you, really look at it before you eat. What textures are there? What are the shapes? What color is it?

Lois, a successful fashion designer, was "totally stressed out" when her well-behaved eleven-year-old twin boys ganged up with her teenage daughter. They refused to do their homework, broke curfew, and created havoc at home. Lois was upset and angry: "all I saw was red." After learning mind-body bridging, she calmed her I-System by focusing on the background colors of the walls, ceiling, sky, and so forth. This rested her I-System, she said, and "I became collected and started making better decisions. Rather than 'seeing red,' I saw clearly what to do."

Pay attention today to what you see when you look at scenery and objects. Notice their colors, shapes, and forms. Pay attention to the facial expressions of the people around you: family, friends, coworkers, and even strangers. When you have a stressful thought, label it "just a thought" and gently return to whatever you were doing. When you really *see* what's out there, your I-System rests, and your appreciation of life expands as your stress level fades.

AWARENESS OF YOUR BODY

The *proprioception system* is an important component of our nervous system that informs us about our posture, movement, and degree of muscle contraction. The tense muscles you experienced in your first exercise were due to the I-System interfering with the proprioception system's natural functioning. Your natural functioning is signaling for the muscle to relax, but your I-System overrides that natural response and tightens up the muscle even further. This is an example of how the I-System works to cause mind-body disharmony. Another example is our response to an injury that causes pain. The acute pain is a signal that immediate action is necessary. After a few minutes, the central nervous system sets up a barrier to reduce the pain signals so you are better able to carry on with your activities. In many patients with chronic pain, the I-System removes the barrier and the intense pain continues for weeks, months, or even years, interfering with their activities and daily lives.

Kim never enjoyed working out and was always happy when it was over. Since learning about mind-body bridging, she turns off her music and pays attention to "my inner music" as she does her resistance and aerobic training. She is aware of the muscles contracting and relaxing and senses their position in space. Not only does she now enjoy the gym, Kim has significantly increased her power and muscle tone.

Let's see how this works. Start leaning slowly to the left—do you feel the muscle tension in your side? Do you sense the imbalance in your head? Do you sense how your natural functioning wants to correct the imbalance? Lift up your right arm and hold it in midair. Do you feel the pull of gravity? Yes, that's your proprioception system at work. It gives you information about the position of your body in space and the state of your muscles. You use that natural flow of information to automatically move and navigate. Pay attention to gravity as you lift an object or as you get up from a chair. Gravity is your friend; it's always there. Sensing gravity quiets the I-System and grounds you in the present moment.

PUTTING IT ALL TOGETHER

Use your stress reduction and power building tools to bust stress, stay relaxed, and stay focused throughout the day. When your thoughts begin to wander from what you are doing, use thought labeling to bring you back. When experiencing stress, use your bridging awareness tools. Notice that your body automatically relaxes and your breathing becomes natural without your having to forcibly adjust it. You are now in direct communication with your mind-body. For example, while cooking, listen to the stove's exhaust fan, and your other senses will automatically open. You smell the soup, you see the colors of the vegetables, and your enjoyment expands.

We all know that driving can be a stressful experience, especially in heavy traffic and construction delays and around unsafe drivers. When driving, keep the radio, music player, and cell phone off. Note what happens to your body tension as you feel the steering wheel, hear the roar and feel the vibrations of the engine, feel the seat belt across your chest, see the scenery, and pay attention to the road. When thoughts pull you away from your driving, label them. Many people have reported to us that these stress reduction and power building tools have literally saved their lives.

When falling asleep tonight, listen to and focus on background sounds. Feel and rub the sheets with your fingers. See the darkness when your eyes are closed. Be patient and keep returning to your senses. The busy head can never settle the busy head. If stressful thoughts keep you awake, label your thoughts. For example, say to yourself, *I'm having the thought "I'll never get to sleep"* or *I'm having the thought "I'm overwhelmed," so what else is new?* and then return to your senses for a good night's sleep. These stress reduction tools (using your senses and thought labeling) stop the I-System's activities from robbing you of restful sleep. The quality of your sleep is a determining factor in maximizing your self-power. If over 90 percent of the people with cancer and/or PTSD in two research studies could improve their sleep using mind-body bridging (Nakamura et al. 2011; Nakamura et al. forthcoming), you can too.

A gentleman with severe sleep problems told us: "I have an old rottweiler who sleeps on my bedroom floor and a young mutt who sleeps on my bed. Now I just listen to the old guy snore and feel the fur of the little guy. I haven't slept so well in twenty years!"

Stress Reduction and Power Building Tools

➤ *Recognizing when your I-System is active or inactive*

➤ *Thought labeling*

➤ *Bridging awareness practices*

   ➤ *Awareness of background sounds*

   ➤ *Awareness of what you are touching*

   ➤ *Awareness of colors, facial features, shapes*

   ➤ *Awareness of your body sensations*

You may ask yourself, *Can labeling my thoughts, listening to background sounds, seeing facial features, feeling my feet on the ground, and being aware of what I touch really relieve stress and build my self-power? Can it really be so simple?* If you consistently use these stress reduction and power building tools, every cell of your body will give you a resounding answer. So, feel your foot as it touches the ground, sense your fingertips on the computer keys, hear the hum of the computer, feel the pressure on your behind as you sit, feel the fork in your hand, look at your food, and be aware of how the broom moves the dust when you sweep. When your thoughts pull you away from your activity, label them and return to what you were doing.

After using these tools for a couple of days, return to this page and fill out the chart and then the following MBB Evaluation Scale.

Stressful Situation	I-System Active or Inactive	Bridging Awareness Tools	Thought Labeling	What Happened
Getting ready for work after oversleeping	Active	Paid attention to the sounds of the shower	I'm having the thought that my boss will be mad	Tension dropped, able to get ready for work calmly

The stronger your mind-body bridging practices, the easier your journey to self-power will be. Have you noticed that the stress reduction and power building tools you're using can be so naturally integrated into your life that they don't take time out of your busy schedule? The MBB Evaluation Scale is a way to gauge your progress and lets you know how solid your foundation is.

MBB EVALUATION SCALE
TAP INTO YOUR SELF-POWER TO CONTROL STRESS

Date: _____

After using the tools in this chapter for several days, check the description that best matches your practice for each question: hardly ever, occasionally, usually, or almost always.

How often do you...	Hardly Ever	Occasionally	Usually	Almost Always
Listen to background sounds?				
Sense the sensations in your fingers when holding your water bottle, coffee cup, cold glass of water, or soda can?				
Sense the sensations in your fingers when you touch things throughout the day?				
Experience pressure on your feet when you walk?				
Experience pressure on your behind as you sit?				
Feel the steering wheel, hear the roar of the engine, and pay attention to the road when driving?				
Hear the water going down the drain and experience it on your body when showering or washing your hands?				
Become keenly aware of everyday activities like making the bed, eating, brushing your teeth, and lifting?				
Become aware of your body sensations when you touch others?				
Become keenly aware of others' facial expressions?				
Use stress reduction and power building tools to help you relax and stay focused at home and at work?				
Use bridging awareness and thought labeling tools to help you sleep?				
Use stress reduction tools to bust stress or melt misery?				
Sense that you are connected to your own wellspring of self-power?				
Recognize when your I-System is active or inactive?				

List two new things you've noticed about your life after starting to use your stress reduction and power building tools:

_____

_____

CHAPTER 2

IMPROVE EVERYDAY LIFE BY RECOGNIZING REQUIREMENTS

Principle: Requirements activate the I-System from its naturally resting state, impairing your executive functioning and creating a stress-filled life.

Principle: Requirement recognition deactivates the I-System, reduces stress, and improves everyday life.

Mind-Body Language:

Requirements: Mental rules your I-System has created for you about how you and the world should be at any moment. Your I-System is activated when these rules are broken.

Requirement recognition: When you become clearly aware that it is *your requirement*, and not the stressor, activating your I-System, you reduce stress and gain self-power.

HOW THE I-SYSTEM WORKS

Many different systems regulate our bodies. For instance, we have a temperature regulation system that keeps our body temperature around 98.6 degrees Fahrenheit. If our temperature goes up, we sweat, and if it goes down, we shiver as our system tries to get back to the body's normal temperature. Similarly, we all have an I-System. It works like our temperature regulation system, but instead of an ideal temperature, the I-System has an "ideal picture" (requirement) of how you and the world should be. Each moment, both systems sense whether the requirements are met. When the temperature regulation system requirement is not fulfilled, we shiver or sweat. When a situation comes up that doesn't fulfill the requirement, our I-System activates, and we have body tension, mind clutter, stress, and impaired functioning.

The natural state of the I-System is to rest. It's only activated when requirements are unfulfilled. Remember, requirements are rules your I-System has created for you about how you and the world should be at any moment (for example, *I should be able to control my stress; my boss shouldn't raise his voice; I should be able to pay my bills*).

It's important to understand the difference between thoughts that are natural expectations and those that are made into requirements. All thoughts are natural and originate free of the I-System's influence. It's not what the thought is about (the content), but what happens to the thought that determines whether or not it's a requirement. For example, *I should have a job* or *she should be faithful* are thoughts or expectations you would naturally have. When the I-System makes them into requirements and a situation violates those requirements, this creates body tension and mental stress and impairs your ability to deal effectively with the situation. When a thought is not a requirement, your mind is clear, your body is relaxed, and you access your self-power. You now have less stress and more power to deal with any situation that may arise. Your days will be more enjoyable and productive.

It's crucial to continually recognize whether or not your I-System is active. For example, someone recklessly cuts in front of you when you're driving. You might think, *He shouldn't drive recklessly—he could have killed me. Is he nuts?* Your hands clench around the steering wheel, you breathe more quickly, your face gets red, and your shoulders go up. You have the telltale signs of an active I-System that's been triggered by the requirement *People shouldn't drive recklessly*. When the I-System takes control of the natural thought or expectation *He shouldn't drive recklessly*, it becomes a requirement. Your blood pressure and stress level rise, impairing your ability to drive safely. Even after the reckless driver has turned off the freeway, your mind remains cluttered with thoughts, and your body is still tense. Your I-System pours salt on the wound by continuing to spin your thoughts and tensing your body, creating even more stress. Your day could be ruined, or even worse, your distress could cause you to have an accident later. It's important to notice that whenever the I-System captures a natural thought or expectation and makes it into a requirement, you become a victim of circumstances because your ability to act appropriately is handicapped.

UNCOVERING REQUIREMENTS

It's time to start mapping your I-System requirements. Remember, the two-part mind-body maps are short written exercises taking only a few minutes. They're vivid snapshots of your thoughts and body tension. Every two-part map you make increases your awareness of your requirements, reduces your I-System's control, and increases your self-power.

1. This mapping exercise is a powerful way to uncover requirements that sap your self-power. Do a How My World Should Be map (see the following sample map). Take a few minutes to scatter around the oval any thoughts you have about how your everyday world should be (for example, *I should have more time for myself,* or *Cris should follow through with his promises*). Be specific, working quickly without editing your thoughts.

HOW MY WORLD SHOULD BE

HOW MY WORLD
SHOULD BE

SAMPLE MAP: HOW MY WORLD SHOULD BE

My house should be
worth more

The economy should be better

I should have more
time for myself

I shouldn't have
to work so hard

HOW MY WORLD
SHOULD BE

Cris should follow
through on his promise

I should be
more relaxed

My kids shouldn't be
so demanding

I should make more money

My spouse shouldn't be
so critical

My partner
shouldn't spend
too much money

I should have a garden

IMPROVE EVERYDAY LIFE BY RECOGNIZING REQUIREMENTS

A. Do you think everything on your map will happen? Yes _____ No _____

B. In this chart, write down each thought and describe your body tension when you realized that it might not happen.

"How My World Should Be" Thought	Body Tension and Location	
Example 1: My partner shouldn't spend too much money.	Churning stomach, tense jaw	√
Example 2: I should have a garden.	Minimal body tension	

C. The body tension you listed is a sign that the thought is a requirement and has activated your I-System. Place a check mark in the third column to indicate that the particular thought is a requirement.

We all have naturally functioning thoughts and expectations about how the world should be. When your I-System captures your thoughts about how the world should be and you realize that it isn't necessarily going to happen, your body tenses, and your mind gets cluttered, creating stress in your life.

Remember, thoughts that trigger your I-System are requirements. In the previous example, take the thought *My partner shouldn't spend too much money*. When you have the thought that your partner spends too much money, your jaw tenses and your stomach churns. This means you have the requirement *My partner shouldn't spend too much money*. If the I-System hadn't captured that thought, it would be a natural expectation instead of a requirement, and you would have been free of stress when you handled the situation, with a ready, relaxed mind and body. For the other thought listed as an example (*I should have a garden*), you have minimal body tension when reality (no garden) doesn't match that thought. In that case, your I-System is not triggered, so the thought *I should have a garden* isn't a requirement, it's a natural thought from executive functioning. It means that if you choose to have or not have a garden, you can do so without stress, with a calm body and clear mind.

2. Now you'll use the bridging awareness practices you learned in chapter 1 and do a How My World Should Be map again. Before you start writing, listen to any background sounds, experience your body's pressure on your seat, sense your feet on the floor, and feel the pen in your hand. Take your time. Once you feel settled, keep feeling the pen in your hand and start writing about how your world should be. Watch the ink go onto the paper, and listen to any background sounds. For the next few minutes, jot down whatever comes to mind about how the world should be.

HOW MY WORLD SHOULD BE WITH BRIDGING

HOW MY WORLD
SHOULD BE

A. What are the differences between this map and the previous map?

_____

_____

B. Do you see that you can face the world as it is, without the pressure and distortion of your I-System that's shown on the previous map that you made? Yes _____ No _____

When a stressor in your life (*My partner spent $2,000 on a new TV*) fills your mind with spinning thoughts and makes your body tense, you know it's your I-System and not the stressor that is causing your distress. Recognize your requirement, tune in to your senses, and you'll no longer have an overactive I-System adding more mind clutter and body tension. You can now handle that situation with a ready, relaxed mind and body. Your stress automatically lessens and your self-power increases.

Whenever you have body tension and mind clutter, it's a sign that one of your I-System's requirements is not being fulfilled. The mapping exercise you have just completed is about increasing your awareness of your requirements. Notice your signs of an overactive I-System. For example, maybe you start to raise your shoulders, your toes curl, you feel overwhelmed, you grip your golf club too tightly, you feel a pain in your neck, you stop hearing the fan, or you slump in your chair. Once you notice a sign, see if you can find the requirement that activated your I-System. When you identify your requirement, you have more control over what's upsetting you. Remember, it is not the situation or another person's behavior that activates your I-System; it's your own requirement.

3. Mull over the stressors you have experienced in the past few days and fill out the chart.

Stressor	Mind Clutter	Body Tension	Requirement
I haven't finished this project and my boss just gave me another one.	I can't get it done, how can he do that to me, he's trying to get rid of me	Shoulder tightness, neck pain, foot tapping	I shouldn't be assigned a new project until I finish the last one.
I'm having a barbecue party and it's supposed to rain.	What will happen if we have to stay in, rain will ruin the party, stupid idea, can't sleep	Headache, jittery, back tight	It shouldn't rain on my party.

Go back over each requirement you listed on the chart. Use your bridging awareness practices and thought labeling and see if you have less stress. Using your stress reduction and power building tools puts you back in charge.

An experienced teacher began having trouble dealing with her large and unruly class, uncooperative parents, and new regulations. Feeling stressed out and at her wits' end, she tried mind-body bridging. She defined her stressors as too few teaching supplies, no district support, class size too big, and being overworked. After recognizing the requirements related to her stressors, she saw another major requirement: *I should be able to handle anything*. Using stress reduction and power building tools, she used thought labeling and tuned in to her senses to calm her I-System. She became aware of what she was holding in her hands, the flavors and textures of what she was eating, and her posture while sitting and standing throughout the day. Her stress level decreased, her tolerance increased, and she even taught her students about rubbing their thumbs gently against their fingers. One student discovered that by rubbing the collar of her jacket near her ear, she could hear and sense something at the same time, helping settle herself down.

STRESSORS

The unexpected is just around the corner, filling life full of stressors. Doing mind-body mapping prepares you to convert whatever stressors you face into self-power. In the following exercise, the first map leads you to clearly identify the requirements connected to your stressors. The second map allows you to experience the mind-body shift from an active I-System to a resting I-System. Mapping consistently reduces your stress and keeps your powerful self in charge.

1. Do a Stressor map. Write down a current stressful problem in the center of the oval. Next, take a couple of minutes to scatter around the oval any thoughts that come to mind. Work quickly, without editing your thoughts. Describe your body tension at the bottom of the map.

STRESSOR MAP

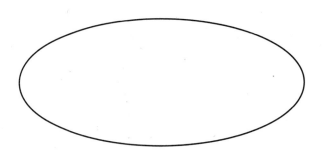

Body Tension: _____

What does your map say about how you are approaching your stressful problem?

A. Is your mind cluttered or clear?

_____

B. Is your body tense or relaxed?

_____

C. What are your requirements?

_____

_____

_____

_____

_____

_____

_____

If your map shows very little sign of an overactive I-System, it may be that you have no requirements, but that's quite unlikely at this point. What's more likely is that your overactive I-System is closing you off, shutting down your normal body sensations.

To find out if that's the case, get out a blank piece of paper and do a map. Put an important thought that brings up no body tension (like *My boss wants to see me tomorrow*) in the oval. Consider that thought to see what comes to mind and write your thoughts around the oval for three to four minutes. Look for body tension on each of the items. Those items that cause body tension help you identify your underlying requirement.

Being unaware of your requirement (*My boss should leave me alone*) keeps your I-System active. The key to reducing stress is recognizing your requirement. You don't have to force yourself to feel anything. Your natural executive functioning will let the process take place gently and powerfully.

2. Using the same stressful problem, do a bridging map, this time using your bridging practices. Write the problem in the oval. Before you start writing, listen to any background sounds, feel your body's pressure on your seat, sense your feet on the floor, and feel the pen in your hand. Take your time. Once you feel settled, keep feeling the pen in your hand and start writing. Watch the ink go onto the paper, and listen to any background sounds. Take a couple of minutes.

STRESSOR MAP WITH BRIDGING

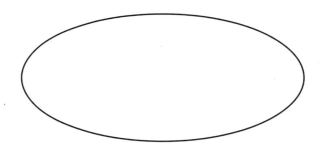

A. Is your mind cluttered or clear?

_____

B. Is your body tense or relaxed?

_____

C. Observe the differences between the two maps:

   i. Are you clearer about your problem? Yes _____ No _____

   ii. In this mind-body state, how would you approach your problem?

_____

_____

   iii. In this mind-body state, do you recognize your ability to reduce stress? Yes _____ No _____

TRIGGERS

Another important method of sharpening your ability to manage stressors without stress overload is to examine triggers. A *trigger* is an event or thought that activates a requirement, heating up your I-System. Any event or thought is a trigger if, and *only* if, that event or thought violates a requirement. Every coin has two sides, and even when flipped, it's still the same coin. Triggers and requirements are the same way. When you become aware of a trigger, it's important to realize that it's pointing you to the requirement (the other side of the coin). Remember, it's not the event or someone else's behavior that activates the I-System; it's your requirement about that event or behavior.

A sixty-five-year-old woman had a disabled and abusive husband. His verbal abuse was always followed by the statement "You deserved that." She knew all along that her husband's abusive behavior triggered a pounding heart, chest pains, headaches, a weighed-down body, and thoughts like *Why me? Why is he like that? How can I put up with this?* Even though she was aware of this, her stress symptoms continued. After learning mind-body bridging, she began recognizing a whole set of requirements related to specific aspects of his behavior: *He shouldn't have that angry look on his face. He shouldn't shout at me. He shouldn't call me names.* By recognizing these requirements, she said, "I somehow felt free. It didn't make sense to me that his clenched blue hands, angry looks, and nasty words would cause my heart to jump out of my chest. I saw the futility of the requirement 'he should be grateful.'" Her stress symptoms decreased, her headaches disappeared, and her energy level improved. As she became more settled by using thought labeling and becoming aware of background sounds, she no longer needed a pounding heart as a signal of an overactive I-System. She knew that whenever her toes curled, "it was a signal to come to my senses and look for my requirements." She became calmer and able to make more appropriate decisions about her life.

1. Jot down on the following table specific trigger behaviors, events, or thoughts that activate your I-System. When someone's behavior toward you is a stressor (mother-in-law's condescending behavior), it's helpful to ask yourself, "What does that look like?" For example, the pitch of her voice, her facial expression, her shaking her finger, the words she uses, her rigid posture.

Trigger Behavior, Event, or Thought	Body Tension and Location
Example 1: My boss's tone of voice	*Jaw tight, clenched fist*
Example 2: I did it wrong.	*Pressure in chest, foot tapping*
Example 3: "That look" from my spouse	*Shoulder muscles tighten*

2. Life is full of situations that most people label as stressors because they cause inner distress and strain your physical and emotional resources. When you clearly recognize the triggers (events, people's behavior, or your own thoughts) that activate your I-System, they will become less stressful. Let's take an up-close-and-personal look at your triggers. Take a few minutes to do a Triggers map by jotting down what triggers your I-System, such as how others behave, demands you make of yourself, or events (for example, *Terry broke his promise, Ann doesn't respect me, I did it wrong, my car broke down, the plane was late*).

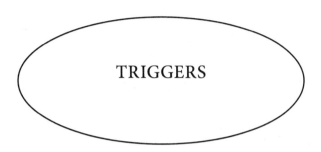

Choose the most stressful items from your map. List these triggers, your associated body tension, and the underlying requirement. Mind-body mapping is always about *your* I-System requirements, not someone else's behavior. Remember that the trigger points to your requirement.

Trigger	Body Tension	Requirement
Terry broke his promise	*Shoulders tight*	*Terry shouldn't break his promise*

USING YOUR BODY AS A COMPASS

Throughout the day, be aware of your body tension. Although the I-System generates body tension and creates stress in your life, it is no more your enemy than a friend who is giving you important information. Awareness of the early signs of body tension lets you know when you are heading in the wrong direction. Use it like a compass (figure 2.1). When you recognize that the I-System is on, know that you are off course. This is when you use your stress reduction and power building tools to quiet its commotion, and your executive functioning will put you on the right course.

A sales representative was traveling to a major corporate meeting. The airline lost her luggage. After promises by the airline to have it delivered in an hour, she went to her hotel, where she showered and waited. Her repeated calls and conversations with the airline officials were useless. She began to panic. The big meeting was only a few hours away and her presentation outfit was in her luggage. Her mind was racing. This signal reminded her of mind-body bridging, and she began feeling her bare feet on the rug as she paced, the lump in her throat, and her tense neck. She then decided to do a two-part Stressor map she titled Lost Suitcase. "The weight of the world came off my shoulders," she said. "Duh! It's me, not my outfit." She arrived ten minutes before the meeting to confer with a colleague. When she stood up to begin her presentation, a different colleague interrupted to ask about her choice of casual attire for a major meeting. Instead of being upset, she calmly described her experience, and her humorous talk, filled with life lessons, "had the whole audience in my hands." She added, "I received a standing ovation."

Remember, when your body is tense and your mind cluttered, your I-System is in the driver's seat. To quiet your I-System, note that it's your requirement, not your stress or the situation, that's causing your distress. Next, listen to any background sounds, sense whatever you're touching, and fully return your awareness to what you were doing.

Headache   Muscle Aches

Tension   Tightness

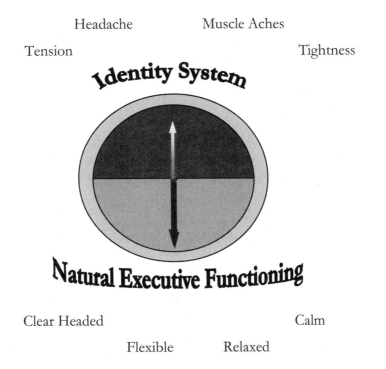

Clear Headed   Calm

Flexible   Relaxed

Figure 2.1: Using Your Body as a Compass

A migratory bird's internal compass tells it when it's veering off course on its way home in the spring. When you recognize your I-System in action, it becomes your compass, letting you know when you are off course. Your awareness is all it takes, because when your I-System is calm, your natural executive functioning automatically lets you effectively navigate daily activities and stressful situations. Use your body as a compass, recognize your requirements, and find your way to your naturally functioning powerful self.

STRESS-DISSOLVING MAP

The What's on My Mind map is one of the most popular and useful stress reduction and power building maps. It can be done anyplace and anywhere, even on a napkin in a coffee shop. This map opens you up as never before to how your mind works. It may seem simple, and you may believe you can do it in your head; however, it's far more powerful to do it in writing. Freely associating on all your maps allows you to be fully in charge of your life.

1. Whenever it's hard to find the underlying requirements, it's helpful to do a What's on My Mind map. Take a couple of minutes to write whatever pops into your mind around the following oval. Work quickly, without editing your thoughts. Your mind produces hundreds of thoughts each minute; the more open you are, the more insight you gain.

> WHAT'S ON MY MIND MAP

WHAT'S ON MY MIND

A. Is your mind cluttered or clear?

_____

B. Is your body tense or relaxed? Describe your body tension:

_____

This is a momentary snapshot of what's on your mind. Notice which thoughts are connected to body tension (for example, *My daughter is acting out, I have to choose which bills to pay, My car needs work*). Recognize the requirement in each thought (*My daughter shouldn't act out; I should be able to pay all my bills; My car shouldn't break down*).

C. What are your requirements?

_____

_____

2. Do this map again, this time using your bridging awareness practices. Before you start writing, listen to any background sounds, feel your body's pressure on your seat, sense your feet on the floor, and feel the pen in your hand. Take your time. Once you feel settled, keep feeling the pen in your hand, and start writing. Watch the ink go onto the paper and listen to any background sounds. For the next few minutes, jot down whatever thoughts pop into your mind.

WHAT'S ON MY MIND MAP WITH BRIDGING

Observe the differences between the two maps:

_____

_____

Remember, thought labeling helps. For example, if you have the thought *My life could be ruined,* say to yourself, *I'm having the thought "My life could be ruined."* What is ruining your life right here, right now isn't losing your job, but the thoughts your I-System has spun about losing the job. You don't have to fix your thoughts, push them away, or force any changes. When the I-System is resting, your executive functioning will automatically help you make decisions about your course of action without the I-System clouding your mind. During the day, being aware that *a thought is just a thought* is all it takes; then you can return your awareness to the task at hand.

PUTTING IT ALL TOGETHER

A contractor was experiencing constant feelings of stress; he was overwhelmed and fearful of his business failing. He was depressed, unsure, and ready to "pack it all in." He even threw his skill saw through a wall when it seized up on a job. After learning mind-body bridging, he used his senses at his job sites by seeing the dust in the air, hearing the construction sounds, and feeling the sensations of his tools in his hands. These bridging awareness practices calmed his I-System so he could recognize the following stressors:

- Customers not paying him as promised

- Overly demanding customers

- Unreliable workers

- Material shortages

- "Subs" not showing up

- Workers cutting corners

When he mapped his stressors and recognized the associated requirements, he reported that "a light-bulb went on. It's not about other people or even about any situation; it's my requirements that are stressing me out! I am not a victim; I'm in control of how I feel and how I act!" With a resting I-System, his stress and anger subsided. He was now able to deal with the challenges on his job, one problem at a time.

Mind-body bridging is an ongoing practice. Use your stress reduction and power building tools to live every aspect of your life with a calm I-System. Your new tools from this chapter are listed below.

Stress Reduction and Power Building Tools

➢ *Using your body as a compass*

➢ *Creating two-part mind-body bridging maps*

➢ *Discovering requirements that activate your I-System*

➢ *Using requirement recognition to quiet your I-System*

MBB EVALUATION SCALE
IMPROVE EVERYDAY LIFE BY
RECOGNIZING REQUIREMENTS

Date: _____

After using the tools in this chapter for several days, check the description that best matches your practice for each question: hardly ever, occasionally, usually, or almost always.

How often do you...	Hardly Ever	Occasionally	Usually	Almost Always
Locate and recognize body sensations as a sign of an overactive I-System?				
Recognize the destructive effects that the I-System has upon your life?				
Recognize that an overactive I-System is underlying your stress?				
Recognize your requirements?				
Catch yourself drifting away from being present in the moment?				
Use bridging awareness practices to quiet the I-System and improve the quality of your life?				
Come to appreciate your life in a different light?				
Do a daily two-part mind-body map?				

When your I-System is overactive, how do you deal with stressors?

_____

_____

When you are using your stress reduction and power building tools and your I-System is at rest, how do you deal with stressors?

_____

_____

What's the most important benefit of doing two-part mind-body bridging maps?

_____

_____

CHAPTER 3

LEARN HOW TO OVERCOME NEGATIVE THINKING

Principle: The depressor keeps your I-System going with troubling thoughts, supporting the powerless self.

Principle: Defusing the depressor restores your self-power, allowing you to overcome stressors.

Mind-Body Language:

Powerless self: How you think, feel, and act when your I-System is overactive. Life is overwhelming, your executive functioning is impaired, and you struggle vainly to keep it all together.

Depressor: A part of the I-System that captures your natural negative thoughts and self-talk and creates body tension and mind clutter.

Storyline: Thoughts spun into stories by your I-System that pull you away from what you are presently doing.

Defusing the depressor: When you become clearly aware (in real time) that your negative thoughts are "just thoughts," those thoughts are then prevented from creating body tension and mind clutter.

THINKING AND NEGATIVE THOUGHTS

Did you know that from the neuroscience viewpoint, a thought is just a secretion, a droplet of chemical where two brain cells connect (synapse)? Did you know that psychologists and others studying the mind sometimes call thoughts *mind facts*? These mind facts are organized, stored, and used as needed to deal effectively with situations as they come up. In this chapter you will discover how your I-System captures thoughts, creates stress, and impairs your abilities.

How your mind thinks and uses thoughts is critical in understanding and overcoming stressors. We know that the mind works dualistically with both positive and negative thoughts. If we have the thought *high*, there must be a *low*; if we think *good*, there must be a *bad*, and the same follows for *happy* and *sad*, *sick* and *well*, and *young* and *old*. Most of us struggle over what to do with our negative thoughts. Many people use positive affirmations to get rid of or deal with their negative thoughts. We have all tried to fix ourselves with positive affirmations, but when we stop, the negative thoughts come back with a vengeance. So what do we do about negative thoughts? Have you noticed that pushing them away only gives them more energy? For example, try not to think of a red balloon. What are you thinking of? A red balloon! The only time we will get rid of our negative thoughts is when we're brain dead.

So the question remains: What do we do with negative thoughts? Our naturally powerful self, which functions in the executive mode, creates harmony and balance out of opposite thoughts. For instance, being sick and being well are both naturally occurring conditions of the mind-body. Your powerful self deals appropriately with each. But the I-System has a totally different approach; its mission is to keep itself going by capturing (usually negative) thoughts. The depressor, a part of the I-System, works by taking your negative thoughts and self-talk (things you say to yourself) and creating body tension and mind clutter. It takes a negative thought like *I'm a loser, I can't do it,* or *I'll never find a job* and weaves a story about that thought, embedding the negativity and stress into every cell of your body. You see yourself as incomplete, powerless, or ruined, and you have a story to prove it! This state is known as the powerless self.

The original question, *What do I do about my negative thoughts?* now becomes *What do I do about my depressor?* The depressor is the doom and gloom of your I-System, using negative self-talk, which naturally arises during the day, to reinforce the powerless self. Today you'll begin to recognize your negative self-talk for what it is, just a thought. Recognition of existing negative thoughts is crucial to your self-power.

Toni, an upbeat sales director for a top pharmaceutical company, was rarely aware of her negative thoughts. She noted that when she felt a "downward dip" in any part of her life, she would "rev up" into her "passing gear" and not look back. However, she eventually began feeling burned out, irritated, and physically exhausted. After two weeks of mind-body bridging, she saw that her negative thoughts were "pushing me to the brink." She became open to thoughts like *I'll never get this done, What if they don't carry through with it?* and *If I don't give it everything I've got, it won't work.* She saw that this negative self-talk was driving her to work eighteen hours a day. Once she learned the tools to deal with her negative self-talk, her stress subsided, she relaxed more, and "the world didn't tumble down."

Try hard to remember your negative self-talk from the past twenty-four hours. On the following chart, note your thoughts and the nature, location, and intensity of any body tension that comes with them (such as headache, stomach cramps, foot tapping, or tight shoulder muscles).

Negative Self-Talk	Body Tension
I'll never get better. I should just give up and accept what is.	*Throat tight, body feels heavy and lethargic, and pressure in chest*

Frank, the CEO of a large multimedia company, denied having negative thoughts. In any crisis, he was only aware of solutions. Frank was oblivious to the connection between his unrecognized negative thoughts and his health. When asked what happened during times of significant stress buildup, he casually stated, "I've been hospitalized three times for bleeding ulcers." To him, it was his high-level job and not his I-System's depressor impacting his health.

The secret to overcoming negative thinking is to understand how the depressor works, how it walls you off from your executive functioning, and how it negatively affects your health. The following maps will give you additional tools to unlock your healing and self-power.

THE DEPRESSOR WEAKENS YOUR SELF-POWER

1. Do a Depressor map. Around the following oval, scatter your negative thoughts and self-talk about a stressful situation or a time when you were bummed out. If any of the thoughts are positive, see if you can identify their negative partners and jot them down (see the sample map on the next page). Write as much as you can for a couple of minutes. Describe your body tension at the bottom of the map.

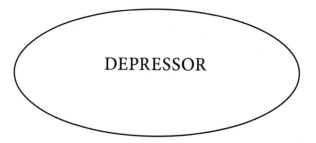

Body Tension: _____

A. What's your behavior like when your depressor is active?

_____

_____

B. Describe the impact on your health and quality of life when your depressor is active:

_____

_____

The thoughts on your map are natural thoughts that happen to be negative. The depressor works by grabbing a negative thought and embedding the negativity in your body, which generates even more negative thoughts. This vicious cycle creates a heavy burden that dramatically reduces your power to handle stressors. The next two maps you create will show you how to manage and defuse your depressor.

SAMPLE MAP: DEPRESSOR

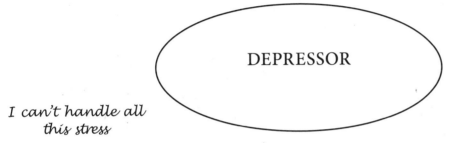

I can't control my life

I'm not good enough

I'm tired of trying

My family doesn't love me

DEPRESSOR

I can't handle all this stress

I can't depend on anyone

I'm worn out

It will be over soon (positive)

↓

It will never end (negative)

I'll find a solution (positive)

↓

I'll never find the right solution (negative)

Body Tension: *clenched jaw, tight shoulders, rumbling stomach, painful neck, heavy body*

43

2. Time to look at your depressor more closely. From your previous Depressor map, take the thought that troubles you the most, creating a lot of body tension (for example, *I'm worn out*) and write it in the following oval. Now, for the next few minutes scatter around the oval any thoughts that come to mind. Use phrases or complete sentences like *Nothing I do works, She doesn't love me,* or *I'll never be able to pay the bills.* Describe your body tension at the bottom of the map.

TROUBLING THOUGHT FROM MY DEPRESSOR MAP

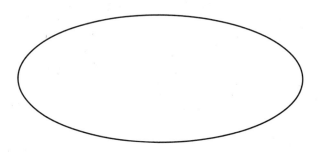

Body Tension: _____

The map you just did holds the key to managing your depressor. The thoughts on your map are spun into stories (true or not) by your I-System. Just think about the stories that come to mind about your negative thoughts. Remember, these are called *storylines*. It's very important to recognize and become aware of their power. Storylines are the link between the negative thoughts that pop into your mind and the mind-body distress you experienced on your last two maps. The I-System's spinning storyline takes a natural negative thought and embeds the negativity into every cell of your body, thereby making a dysfunctional mind-body connection. Storylines keep the I-System going, taking you away from the present moment. Stopping the depressor's storylines keeps negative thoughts from causing distress.

3. Use your bridging awareness practices and do the previous map again. Write the same troubling thought in the oval. Before you continue, listen to background sounds, feel your body's pressure on your seat, sense your feet on the floor, and feel the pen in your hand. Take your time. Once you feel settled, keep feeling the pen in your hand and start writing. Watch the ink go onto the paper, and listen to background sounds. Write for a couple of minutes.

TROUBLING THOUGHT FROM MY DEPRESSOR MAP WITH BRIDGING

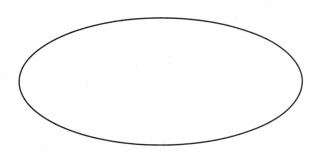

Notice the differences between the two maps:

A. Is your mind cluttered or clear?

_____

B. Is your body tense or relaxed?

_____

C. In this mind-body state, how do you handle stressors?

_____

_____

STEPS TO DEFUSE YOUR DEPRESSOR

When you feel down and have body tension, use the following tools to defuse your depressor so your naturally powerful self, functioning in the executive mode, is back in the driver's seat:

1. Recognition of the depressor: Recognize that whenever your mind has negative thoughts *and* you have body tension, it's your depressor and not the thoughts, situation, or event that is causing your distress.

2. Thought labeling: Thought labeling is the first tool you use to gain control over troubling thoughts. Choose a thought from one of your maps that still creates body tension. Say slowly to yourself, *I am having the thought* [*insert your thought*]. Are you sensing a reduction of body tension? Remember, it's your depressor and not the content of your thoughts that causes your distress.

3. Bridging awareness practices: If you still feel body tension after using the steps above, listen to background sounds and feel your behind on the chair and your feet on the ground. Do you experience a reduction of body tension? If so, you have defused your depressor.

A lieutenant colonel in the army twice failed the qualifying exam to become a full colonel. She hesitated to take the four-hour exam again because if she failed this time, she would have to leave the army. Her I-System's depressor created story after story, keeping her from moving forward. She reported that during the exam her brain would shut down; she couldn't think and couldn't find the correct multiple-choice answers. After using the stress reduction and power building tools in this workbook, she prepared for the exam by practicing her bridging awareness tools, thought labeling, recognizing her storylines and depressor, and mapping her requirements, rather than reviewing the material, which she already knew. She recognized the requirements *I should pass the test* and *I should be a colonel*. All of her life, her value as a human being had been dependent upon fulfilling her requirements. She smiled in relief when she *recognized* that the test and her promotion were not an evaluation of who she was. She finished the four-hour exam in one hour and forty-five minutes and scored 98 percent.

STORYLINE AWARENESS SETS YOU FREE

Another powerful stress reduction tool is storyline awareness. Remember, storylines are thoughts spun into stories that keep your I-System active. Storylines aren't just stories; they have a destructive physical effect on your body and cloud your reality. The negative storylines tend to define us, and the positive ones tend to confine us. All storylines lead us into the past or future. This takes you away from being present in the moment and effectively handling the stressor at hand. Storyline awareness is simply recognizing the storyline, realizing the damage it's doing, and letting your awareness interrupt the story. Your executive functioning is automatically restored.

Joseph, a thirty-year-old software engineer had moved to Seattle from Los Angeles, to take a new job. His new job was going very well, but he couldn't understand why he was becoming depressed. He even lost interest in going to the gym or having a social life. He kept going over memories of how great the weather was in L.A. and how much fun he had had under those sunny skies. Joseph started comparing his life then to his life now. His depressor's negative self-talk and stories were all about Seattle's gloomy weather: *Those gray clouds. All it does is rain. How can people stand it?* Months went by; even using a high-tech light box (suggested by a friend) improved his mood only slightly. After learning mind-body bridging, he began quieting his I-System by *seeing* the gray of the sky, hearing the raindrops, and feeling the humidity on his skin. He later remarked, "I was trying hard to push away my negative thoughts about the bleak weather, but it didn't work. When I visualized the weather in L.A., it only made things worse. Now when I start running my stories about L.A. and Seattle, I know my I-System is active. I recognize my storylines, recognize my requirement as *The weather in Seattle should be as nice as L.A.'s*, and quiet my I-System, putting my executive-functioning self back in control. I'll never be a victim of the weather again."

By using your storyline awareness tool (just being aware of the storyline) during the day, you'll see how much of your time storylines swallow up. You don't need to push the story away; you just need to become aware of it. Your awareness dissolves the storyline and will even help you sleep better at night.

An Olympic figure skater favored to win a gold medal looked at her coach for guidance before going out on the ice. Seeing the tension on her face, the coach told her, "Remember, you're a great skater—you can do it. You've done this routine hundreds of times. Just go over how many successes you've had." All went well until she fell on her second jump. The rest of the performance didn't improve. What happened? The skater's depressor was overactive, generating negative storylines, which the coach had tried to fix with positive storylines. With her I-System active, the skater lost touch with the present moment, her senses dulled, and she lost her feel for the ice. If her coach had been trained in mind-body bridging, his instructions to his skater would have been quite different. He would have reminded her to use her senses to stay in the moment: to hear the sound of her skates on the ice, feel the air move past her face and body, and experience the tight lacing of her skates. She would have been able to calm her I-System and may well have won a gold medal.

Think back over the past week, observe how your I-System wove negative storylines, and note the hidden requirements. Fill out the chart below.

Situation	Negative Self-Talk	Storylines	Requirement
I don't have a job.	I'm not smart enough for today's jobs.	I'll never get a job because the economy is bad. I'm not trained well enough.	I should have a job.

Start mulling over one of your most powerful storylines and try to keep it going. Now become aware of background sounds. While continuing to listen to those sounds, observe how your storyline unfolds. Is the storyline running out of gas? Continuing to use your bridging awareness practices weakens your storylines.

THE STRESS OF "WHAT IF"

When her ex-husband suddenly decided to seek custody of their daughter, a happily remarried woman began to experience headaches and insomnia and started overeating. He had invented many stories claiming that she was an unfit mother and was harming their daughter. As she became depressed, her negative self-talk and storylines kept her in "a never-ending series of 'what if's that were paralyzing me and preventing me from living my everyday life even though I knew deep down that the truth would come out." After learning mind-body stress reduction and power building tools, she did numerous two-part What If maps. Her recognition of her storylines, which were keeping her I-System's depressor going, dramatically improved her symptoms. As she continued using her tools, her executive functioning allowed her to make better decisions. She began sleeping better and living a healthier life. During the six months of legal hassles, her life at home and at work was better than *before* her ex came back into the picture.

1. The following maps take a look at those "what if's" that create distress whenever you think about them or even try to not think about them. Do a What If map. Take a couple of minutes to scatter around the oval any "what if" thoughts that come to mind about important situations in your life that may have a negative outcome (see the sample map on the following page). Work quickly, without editing your thoughts. Describe your body tension at the bottom of the map.

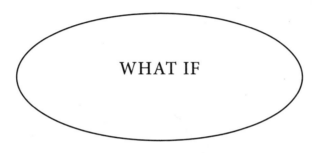

Body Tension: _____

A. Is your mind cluttered or clear?

_____

B. List your depressors and storylines:

_____

_____

C. List your requirements:

_____

_____

D. In this mind-body state, how do you handle stressors?

_____

SAMPLE MAP: WHAT IF

I get sick

I die early
in life

I lose my house

He finds out the truth

My daughter doesn't
get better grades

WHAT IF

I give in to my pain

My husband doesn't
stop smoking

My mother doesn't recover
from surgery

I can't find a job that pays better

I don't complete my life's work

I can't get a good night's sleep

My company goes
bankrupt

Body Tension: *knots in shoulders, band around head, stomach flip-flops, heavy body*

2. Use your bridging awareness practices and do the map again. Before you continue, listen to background sounds, feel your body's pressure on your seat, sense your feet on the floor, and feel the pen in your hand. Take your time. Once you feel settled, keep feeling the pen in your hand and start writing. Watch the ink go onto the paper, and listen to background sounds. Write for a couple of minutes.

WHAT IF MAP WITH BRIDGING

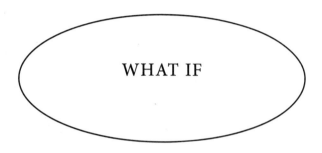

Notice the differences between the two maps:

A. Is your mind cluttered or clear?

_____

B. Is your body tense or relaxed?

_____

C. In this mind-body state, how do you handle stressors?

_____

_____

RESOLVING YOUR MOST DISTRESSING "WHAT IF"

1. Most of us have an underlying "what if" that makes us sick to our stomach whenever we think about it (*What will happen to the kids if I die? What if I don't complete my life's work? What if my company goes bankrupt?*). Do another map using any "what if" that still troubles you. Write the item in the oval. Next, take a couple of minutes to scatter around the paper any thoughts that come to mind. Work quickly, without editing your thoughts. Describe your body tension at the bottom of the map.

MOST DISTRESSING WHAT IF MAP

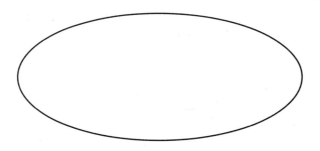

Body Tension: _____

A. Is your mind cluttered or clear?

_____

B. Is your body tense or relaxed?

_____

C. List your depressors and storylines:

_____

_____

D. List your requirements:

_____

_____

E. In this mind-body state, how do you handle stressors?

_____

2. Using your bridging awareness practices, do the previous map again. Write the same troubling item in the oval. Before you continue, listen to background sounds, feel your body's pressure on your seat, sense your feet on the floor, and feel the pen in your hand. Take your time. Once you feel settled, keep feeling the pen in your hand and start writing. Watch the ink go onto the paper, and listen to background sounds. Write for a couple of minutes.

MOST DISTRESSING WHAT IF MAP WITH BRIDGING

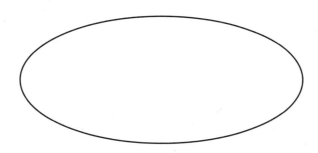

Notice the differences between the two maps:

A. Is your mind cluttered or clear?

_____

B. Is your body tense or relaxed?

_____

C. In this mind-body state, how do you handle stressors?

_____

_____

SEVEN KEY QUESTIONS TO HELP YOU OVERCOME NEGATIVE THOUGHTS

Answer the following questions when your negative thoughts are getting you down.

1. What are the signals that your depressor is overactive? (*heavy body, knot in stomach, thoughts that I'm not good enough*)

   _____

2. What is your behavior like? (*become cranky, want to be left alone, drink too much, work harder, try to be more optimistic, try to use positive affirmations*)

   _____

3. How is it interfering with your executive functioning? (*I'm not making good decisions, my parenting is inconsistent, I let stress control me, I feel enormous pressure to succeed*)

   _____

4. Do you experience yourself as losing control of your life? Yes _____ No _____ How so?

   _____

   _____

5. What are your storylines? (When captured by your I-System, the thought *My life is too hard* is spun into these storylines: *No matter how hard I work, nothing seems to go my way; I try and try, but no one gives me a break; I'm always in the wrong place at the wrong time; I should be able to do what I want for a change.*)

   _____

6. Are these thoughts and storylines creating who you are? Yes _____ No _____ How so?

   _____

7. What are your requirements? (*My life should be easier, I should get things done, I should be the person I want to be, I shouldn't be worn out, I should be able to control the stress*)

   _____

   _____

Your depressor interferes with your executive natural functioning, making you see yourself as powerless, and limits your ability to act.

PUTTING IT ALL TOGETHER

Lucy, a single mother, was working two jobs to support her children. Worries about how to manage all her responsibilities kept her from getting a good night's sleep. In the morning, she would wake up with thoughts about being overwhelmed, which made it harder to get through the day. Several weeks after learning mind-body bridging, she reported, "Sometimes I still wake up in the morning with the thought *I can't do it*, but now I say to myself, *I am having the thought "I can't do it," so what else is new?* On the way to the bathroom, if I start to weave a storyline, I just become aware of it while listening to the fan's humming, and feel the pressure on my feet as I walk. By the time I get to the bathroom, I'm no longer filled with tension and resentment. I don't even need to tell myself positive stories about how I'm a survivor. What I found for myself, by myself, was that it wasn't my situation in life that was preventing a good night's sleep and stressing me out in the morning; it was my storylines. My depressor used to make me feel stressed out by filling my mind and body with negative thoughts. Now even though I still have two jobs, I'm no longer stressed about it!"

Let's look at the stress reduction and power building tools Lucy used to defuse her depressor.

1. She recognized it was her depressor and not her stressful thoughts overwhelming her.

2. She used thought labeling to get control of her negative thoughts.

3. She became aware that the spin of her storylines filled her with tension and resentment.

4. She used her bridging awareness tools to calm her I-System and gain access to her innate wisdom and power.

Below are the three new tools discussed in this chapter. Use them with the tools you learned in the previous two chapters to defuse your depressor and access your self-power.

Stress Reduction and Power Building Tools

> ➤ *Recognizing the depressor's activity*
>
> ➤ *Storyline awareness*
>
> ➤ *Defusing the depressor*

MBB EVALUATION SCALE
LEARN HOW TO OVERCOME NEGATIVE THINKING

Date: _____

After using the tools in this chapter for several days, check the description that best matches your practice for each question: hardly ever, occasionally, usually, almost always.

How often do you...	Hardly Ever	Occasionally	Usually	Almost Always
Recognize negative self-talk and body tension as a sign of the depressor?				
Notice that your depressor is running wild and making you feel helpless and powerless?				
Locate body sensations linked to the depressor?				
Experience the beneficial effects of defusing your depressor by staying aware of its activity during the day and using thought labeling?				
Recognize storylines?				
Experience that the powerless self comes from your I-System and is a myth?				
Recognize natural executive functioning when your I-System is resting?				

List the main body tensions you notice accompanying the depressor:

_____

List the themes of two storylines:

_____

_____

List two behaviors that are associated with the depressor:

_____

_____

What's it like to defuse your depressor and function with a resting I-System?

_____

_____

CHAPTER 4

REACH YOUR GOALS WITHOUT STRESS

Principle: The I-System's fixer is the driving force that pushes you to make everything perfect in your life, but instead it creates added stress, impairs your performance, and restricts your ability to take care of yourself and your responsibilities.

Principle: Defusing the fixer during an activity immediately reduces stress, and your powerful self performs that activity.

Mind-Body Language:

Fixer: The depressor's partner that drives you with overactive, never-ending thoughts of how to fix yourself and the world.

Defusing the fixer: When you become clearly aware (during an activity) that your fixer is active and use your stress reduction and power building tools, you take away the fixer's power. You immediately experience a shift from a stressful, driven state to one with a ready and relaxed mind and body. You can now actively and assertively take care of yourself and your responsibilities in the executive functioning mode.

Depressor/fixer cycle: These I-System partners create a vicious cycle, stop you from reaching your goals, and keep the I-System going and going.

THE HIDDEN ENEMY WITHIN: THE FIXER

What price have you paid for your accomplishments? Have you spent enough time with your family? How's your headache? What about your ulcer, or your IBS? How's your back doing? How else has your body suffered during your struggle to reach your goals? What else have you sacrificed?

Look at all of your accomplishments. Have you ever wondered why that sense of satisfaction doesn't last long? Why does your mind always find higher mountains to climb? You may believe that without feeling driven, without experiencing mental pressure and having a tense body, you cannot achieve success. By the end of this chapter, you'll experience your path to success without stress overload and with a sense of satisfaction.

Let's talk about that long list of self-improvement goals: refusing that extra cookie, exercising, spending more time with family and loved ones, having fun, procrastinating less, staying relaxed, feeling less stress, being better disciplined, making better decisions, finding the right career, and landing the perfect job. How successful have you been? How long did your efforts last? Were they just this year's batch of New Year's resolutions? Were you confident that if you could fix yourself, you would have less stress and make a better life? Trying to learn a specialized technique to deal with each item is time consuming and never ends.

In this chapter, you'll discover the main reason your attempts have failed, or why you have paid such a high price for success. Time to meet the *fixer*. The fixer's job is to make you *think* it is helping you by pushing you to "try harder" and "be stronger" while filling you with body tension.

The fixer is the I-System's helper and the depressor's lifelong, faithful partner. Your fixer comes up with never-ending thoughts and storylines that focus on how to fix you and the world. Your fixer brings a sense of urgency and pressure to your activities, and when it's in play, enough is never going to be enough. The fixer starts from the false belief that you are broken, tries to fix you, and works by making you believe it's really helping you. You can recognize the fixer by noticing your increased body tension and a mind full of thoughts like *Try harder, Do more, Be smarter,* or *Be stronger.* No matter what you accomplish, the depressor jumps in with thoughts like *not good enough,* further activating your fixer. The depressor and fixer work together (depressor/fixer cycle), keeping the I-System going and leading to the disruptive mind-body state, the powerless self.

For instance, rather than give in to his symptoms, Jim, a veteran recently returned from Afghanistan, declared war on them. As soon as he saw any sign of helplessness or weakness, he immediately pushed himself to try harder, but his efforts fell far short of his expectations. Whatever he tried to do, enough was never enough, causing even more mind clutter and body tension. No matter how hard he tried or how well he did, his inner tension never went away. He couldn't "fix" himself.

Jim didn't know his fixer was in the driver's seat. He believed his stress and lack of healing were a "normal" part of his life and that time would heal all wounds. His combat experiences activated his I-System, and his stress-related symptoms caused him to experience himself as damaged. Despite Jim's best efforts, his fixer never fixed his powerless self.

Using mind-body bridging tools (stress reduction and power building), Jim began noticing his body tension and mental pressure and realized his I-System's fixer was active. He saw the stress and strain the fixer caused, which was difficult at first because trying harder, fighting, and overcoming obstacles were part of his nature. However, he soon felt the extra tension that came with his fixer and recognized that the "fixing" was never-ending. But most important, he found that for every fixer thought (for example, *Be stronger* or *Be successful*), there was an embedded depressor thought (for example, *I'm weak* or *I'm a failure*). He saw clearly that what motivated him was his fixer, because no matter how many successes he had, he never found peace of mind or a sense of well-being. During his daily activities, whenever his chest tightened, he realized it was the telltale sign of his fixer activity. Using his mind-body bridging tools in his everyday life, he drove himself less and accomplished more. His stress-related symptoms began decreasing. Jim was learning to have his powerful self, functioning in the executive mode, in charge.

All of your actions throughout the day are either fixer driven or examples of executive functioning. During an activity, recognize the difference between the two, defuse your I-System's fixer, and reach your goals without added stress. Your naturally powerful self, functioning in the executive mode, is now in charge.

MEET YOUR FIXER

It's a natural aspiration to want to improve our lives and accomplish our goals, so it's critical to recognize when the fixer is in control. The following fixer map is really going to surprise you. Around the oval, jot down the thoughts that come up about "How I Am Going to Improve My Life." Work quickly for a couple of minutes, without editing your thoughts.

HOW I AM GOING TO
IMPROVE MY LIFE

A. Looking at your overall map, how do you feel? Calm _____ Tense _____ Overwhelmed _____

The statements on your map may be either fixer thoughts from an active I-System or natural thoughts from executive functioning about taking care of yourself and your responsibilities. For all your efforts and good intentions to succeed, it's important to know which of your daily activities the fixer is capturing. One way to do this is to consider each item on your map and figure how much body tension you have when you think about going for this self-improvement goal.

B. Next to each item on your map, note your level of body tension using one of these symbols: Ø for no body tension, + for mild, ++ for moderate, or +++ for severe. It may help to see the sample map at the end of the exercise.

The thoughts that come with body tension are your fixer thoughts, and the thoughts with no body tension are from executive functioning. Your challenge is telling the difference between the two. Body tension that comes with thoughts means your fixer is active. The fixer also brings a mental urgency, creating extra pressure for you to act. Remember, executive functioning is how you think, feel, see the world, and act when your I-System is resting. When you are in the executive functioning mode and don't reach a goal, you're naturally disappointed. But when you don't reach a fixer goal, you feel devastated; your mind spins with thoughts and your body is tense.

C. Look over each item on your map again, and note the body tension when you imagine that you're not going to reach that goal. What happens? If you now feel body tension and mind clutter, those items are also fixer thoughts. List all your fixer thoughts from this map:

_____

_____

_____

D. List thoughts on this map that are from executive functioning:

_____

_____

E. It's important to compare this Fixer map with the Depressor map in chapter 3:

   i. Which map has the higher overall energy levels (makes you feel better)?

   Depressor map _____   Fixer map _____

Elevated energy levels that come with the fixer (and make you feel better) aren't unusual. This higher endorphin level can keep you from recognizing the fixer, because you feel good about the thoughts. When active, the fixer impairs your judgment and affects your actions. Thoughts on this map, when fixer driven (*Impress my boss with my abilities, Be a better parent*), can set you up for overwork, risky thrill-seeking activities, or even addictions.

   ii. Your body is always giving you helpful information. Note the differences in location, quality, and intensity of the body tension that comes with the thoughts on the Depressor and Fixer maps (for example, *My body tension on the Depressor map was located around my gut, and my body felt heavy and unresponsive* or *On my Fixer map, my body tension is around my chest and head, and there's a jittery feeling*).

_____

_____

The intensity of your body tension and the driving pressure of your storylines are important signs that your fixer is active. Storylines are a sign that your fixer is restricting your ability to deal with your current activity stress free.

SAMPLE MAP: HOW I AM GOING TO IMPROVE MY LIFE

Be more creative Ø

Impress my boss with my abilities ++

Be in more control +++

Be a better parent +++

HOW I AM GOING TO IMPROVE MY LIFE

Go to the gym 4 times a week ++

Eat less and healthier ++

Manage my money more wisely +

Create better teamwork through activities Ø

Have more free time +++

Fixer thoughts are those that come with body tension when you think about trying to reach your self-improvement goals (for example, *Be a better parent, Eat less, Impress my boss with my abilities, Be more in control, Go to the gym four times a week, Have more free time*). Also note any thoughts from natural functioning (without body tension, marked Ø; for example, *Be more creative* and *Create better teamwork through activities*).

THE MASK OF THE FIXER

The mask of the fixer takes many forms. For instance, George mowed his lawn two to three times a week. He always tried to make it perfect because it was "never good enough." Mari was on an endless merry-go-round, left exhausted from busily meeting her children's needs. Connie drove herself so hard at work that she needed medicine to lower her blood pressure. Ray tried so hard to be a "good husband" that his wife almost left him. Larry's stressors so overwhelmed him that he tried to "fix" himself with a bottle of whiskey a day. Lynn loved driving very fast because it made her feel alive. Tia would push herself relentlessly because she was never satisfied with her life. Al was so competitive that no victory was ever enough, and he was even driven to compete with his teenage son. And Judi was so fixated on staying young that it was affecting her relationship with her daughter.

The fixer triggers mental pressure, urging you to act. It can either drive your actions or leave you feeling overwhelmed and restricted. Be aware of the way your fixer frames the demand. The fixer traps you into thinking, *I need to, I have to, I must*, or *I should*. When your I-System is switched on and the fixer is in the driver's seat, it can drive activities that are difficult for you to control: overeating, drinking too much, taking substances, lying, and taking shortcuts. The fixer clouds your judgment, pushing you to do what relieves your tension or provides instant gratification. At the time, you may feel you made the right choice, but later you're regretful. You ignored the law of cause and effect because your fixer kept you unaware of the consequences of your choice. Whenever your fixer is active, you experience body tension, storylines, and mental pressure. Note how your fixer pushes your behavior.

The fixer will mask itself as the great savior in your life. At first the fixer seems to improve your life and appears helpful. Remember, the fixer's real job is to fix how the depressor makes you feel and keep the I-System going. This strengthens the powerless self. It's the ultimate paradox! At times, the fixer uses positive thoughts like *Exercise more, Eat better, Sleep better, Work harder, Enjoy life*, or *Be a better parent*, hiding the underlying depressor thoughts *I'm fat, I eat wrong, I don't take care of myself, I'm lazy, I don't deserve to have fun*, or *I'm a bad parent*. When the fixer uses thoughts like *Pass everyone on the road, Punch out that son of a bitch, Have that bottle of wine*, and *Escape from this stress*, it can be easier to recognize the negative implications and destructive powers of the fixer.

But, never underestimate the *pressure* the fixer creates when trying to fix the powerless self. For example, the urge to overeat, drink, or take drugs is the fixer trying to fix how the depressor makes you feel. It creates so much pressure, tension, and mental turbulence that it clouds your ability to recognize the consequences of your actions. The destructive consequence of your overindulgence activates your depressor, and your fixer then pushes you to overindulge again, creating a stressful yo-yo effect (depressor/fixer/depressor/fixer…). The fixer can also masquerade as a helper by pushing you to diet, stop drinking, or stop taking drugs. Even when these attempts seem positive, they fail because they are carried out with an active I-System and not by the powerful self in the executive functioning mode. To break this cycle, become actively aware of the fixer's mental and physical pressure that's driving your activity and recognize your underlying depressor.

YOUR FIXER HAS AN UNDERLYING DEPRESSOR

1. Every fixer has an embedded depressor that is driving it. Look again at your Fixer map, "How I Am Going to Improve My Life." Write down your embedded depressor thoughts under the fixer thoughts. See the following sample map.

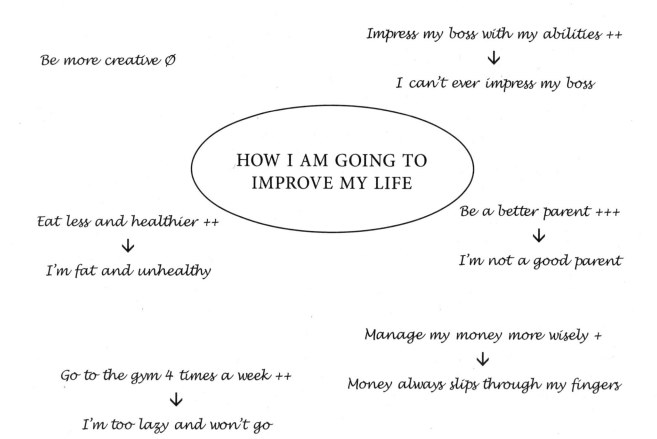

SAMPLE MAP: HOW I AM GOING TO IMPROVE MY LIFE MAP WITH DEPRESSOR THOUGHTS

Impress my boss with my abilities ++
↓
I can't ever impress my boss

Be more creative ∅

HOW I AM GOING TO IMPROVE MY LIFE

Eat less and healthier ++
↓
I'm fat and unhealthy

Be a better parent +++
↓
I'm not a good parent

Manage my money more wisely +
↓
Money always slips through my fingers

Go to the gym 4 times a week ++
↓
I'm too lazy and won't go

Create better teamwork through activities ∅

2. Think about last weekend. The fixer is always active when you attempt to escape from how the depressor makes you feel. Note below any of your activities that created mental or physical pressure (fixer activity). Can you find the embedded depressor activity? Note your stress level with Ø for none, + for mild, ++ for moderate, or +++ for severe.

Fixer Activity	Stress Level	Depressor Activity	Storyline
Maxed out my credit card	++	I feel empty and depressed.	It's just shopping therapy.
Drank too much	+++	Overwhelmed with stress	I deserve to relax.
Yelled at my kids	++	They will never listen to me.	They won't listen.
Gambling, risky investments	+++	I feel drained and empty.	I need excitement.
Excessive computer gaming, porn	++	I'm tense and miserable.	I must reduce my tension.
Clicking a pen	++	Can't stand this anymore, ready to explode	I wish he would stop talking.

A. When your fixer was active, what were the consequences of your behavior? (Outcomes for *drank too much*: got sick, missed work, spent my rent money)

_____

_____

B. What was the common underlying requirement you were trying to meet?

_____

To stop the fixer/depressor cycle and reduce the stress in your life, you need to recognize and defuse the embedded depressor. With a resting I-System, your naturally powerful self, functioning in the executive mode, will be in charge of your work, relationships, and recreational activities.

YOU ARE NOT BROKEN AND DON'T NEED FIXING

Mike, being hard driven and very successful, rapidly reached the top of the corporate ladder. The more success Mike achieved, the more his I-System falsely convinced him that he was on the right track, that he should just keep going and never let up on himself. Although he had everything he had always dreamed of, something was still missing, and his sense of accomplishment never lasted very long. "It's like I'm first across the finish line, expecting booming applause and all I get is deadening silence. With all my hard work, I finally reach for that golden ring and all I get is an arm pulled out of joint. In the past if I felt down, I would work harder and create new goals to motivate me, thinking when I finally achieved them, I would feel successful. I didn't." Having developed hypertension, he was referred for mind-body bridging by his primary care physician. He gradually integrated the bridging awareness practices and thought-labeling tools into his everyday life. As a result, his blood pressure started to go down. However, it was the fixer maps that transformed his life. Naturally organized and a leader, he was gifted at creating more and more value for the customer and motivating people. When his fixer latched on to his natural gifts, enough was never enough. He saw that his storylines and the emptiness and depressive feelings he now felt were really present all along and kept driving his fixer, affecting his health. After putting all of his stress reduction and power building tools together, he defused his fixer by becoming aware of the mental pressure, smiling at his fixer thoughts, and carrying on with his activities with a calm body and clear mind. In addition to lowering his systolic blood pressure by twenty points, he began to enjoy his work and play. Mike grinned as he said, "I still set the highest bar, and now I can enjoy every minute of it!"

The only time you can defuse and stop your fixer is in the moment, while your I-System is active. When you stop the depressor/fixer cycle and calm your I-System, your powerful self controls the activity in the executive functioning mode. Throughout the day notice the activity of your fixer: the depressor/fixer cycle, storylines, body tension, and mental pressure.

When your fixer is active, use these steps to defuse it:

1. During an activity, notice any body tension, mental pressure, and spinning storylines pushing you. These point to your fixer.

2. Use bridging awareness practices and thought labeling to quiet your I-System.

3. Be on the lookout for new stories that the I-System's fixer (or embedded depressor) may spin about how the fixer can help you. These storylines impair your judgment and cause you to act in a way that makes you feel regretful afterward.

4. Recognize the underlying depressor and realize that the fixer's real motive is to repair the powerless self (the fixer can't fix the powerless self, because the fixer keeps the I-System going).

5. Remember, it's not the activity you are doing, it's who's doing it that matters, your powerless self or your powerful self.

You know when you have defused your fixer because your I-System is quiet, your body is calm, and your activities are being done by your powerful self and not the pressure-driven fixer. You witness first-hand that the powerless self is a false belief caused by your active I-System. You are not broken and don't need fixing.

WHY ARE YOUR TO-DO'S OVERWHELMING?

You may become exhausted thinking about the never-ending list of to-do's. The following map shows you how to approach your responsibilities with executive functioning rather than the I-System's fixer.

1. Around the oval, jot down all the things you need to get done over the next few days. Write for a couple of minutes, without editing your thoughts.

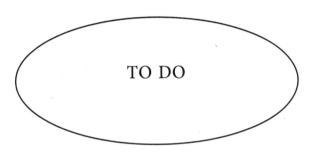

A. Next to each item on your map, note your level of body tension using one of these symbols: Ø for no body tension, + for mild, ++ for moderate, or +++ for severe. It may help to see the sample map that follows. Those items with body tension are fixers.

B. List the storylines associated with the three fixers with the most body tension:

_____

_____

_____

SAMPLE MAP: TO DO

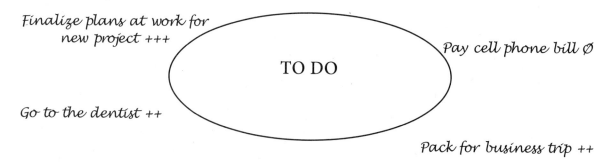

Prepare for tomorrow's meeting ++

Finalize plans at work for
new project +++

Pay cell phone bill Ø

TO DO

Go to the dentist ++

Pack for business trip ++

Get to work early tomorrow +

Go to the parent-
teacher conference +++

Call Mom +++

Get car serviced ++

Go for a run +

Sample storylines:

A.   Call Mom: I should call her now. Maybe she'll leave me alone. Knowing her, she'll call me all weekend wanting me to drive her around. Why does this happen every weekend?

B.   Go to the parent-teacher conference: Charlie won't do his homework, and I can't do anything about it. He lies about his grades. I feel guilty. The teacher will think I'm a bad parent.

C.   Finalize plans at work for new project: I need to do more work at home or it won't be done right. My boss demands too much from me. I am really anxious I'll get fired if it isn't right.

2. Let's do the map again, this time using your bridging awareness practices, and see what happens. Before you start writing, listen to background sounds, feel your body's pressure on your seat, sense your feet on the floor, and feel the pen in your hand. Take your time. Once you're settled, keep feeling the pen in your hand, and start writing. Scatter your thoughts around the oval. Watch the ink go onto the paper, and listen to background sounds. Write for a couple of minutes.

TO DO MAP WITH BRIDGING

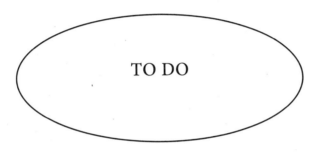

A. Compare the two maps. What do you notice?

_____

B. In this mind-body state, how do you experience your to-do list now?

_____

_____

The release of body tension and the reduction of mind clutter and sense of urgency mean that you have shifted into executive functioning. You discovered that it was the fixer/depressor cycle, with its related storylines, that has been overwhelming you, not your responsibilities. Without the I-System adding any stress or taking away any power, you manage your responsibilities more effectively and naturally.

Now that you have calmed your I-System and freed yourself from its burden, it's time for you to take care of your to-do list functioning in the executive mode.

WHY GOALS ARE HARD TO REACH

1. Self-power means you have the ability to achieve your goals without stress and with a sense of well-being. This exercise will prepare you to accomplish goals that have been difficult. Select a particular goal that has been difficult to achieve (for example, *Getting into better shape*), and write it in the oval. For several minutes, jot down around the oval any thoughts that come up about that goal.

GOAL MAP

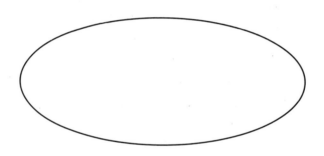

A. For each thought on your map, write in the table below the type and location of any body tension and the amount of mental pressure you feel when you think about trying to reach your goal.

B. Identify and list the embedded depressor thought and requirement for each thought.

Fixer Thought	Body Tension	Mental Pressure	Depressor Thought	Requirement
I'm going to try harder to lose weight.	*Chest and gut tight*	++	*I'm fat.*	*I should be slim.*

C. Did you recognize the storylines that kept your depressor and fixer dancing? What were some of them?

_____

_____

_____

_____

Your fixer thoughts are the response to your depressor's demands, driving you to meet your I-System's requirements. When the I-System isn't activated by requirements, it's resting. However, once an event or condition triggers the I-System by not meeting one of its requirements, the fixer, the depressor, and the storylines create the energy (commotion) that keeps the I-System going. This process makes it difficult for you to achieve your goals.

2. You just experienced your I-System's resistance, preventing you from accomplishing your goal. Let's do the map again, this time using your bridging awareness practices, and see what happens. Write the same goal in the oval. Before you start writing, listen to background sounds, feel your body's pressure on your seat, sense your feet on the floor, and feel the pen in your hand. Take your time. Once you're settled, keep feeling the pen in your hand, and start writing. Scatter your thoughts around the oval. Watch the ink go onto the paper, and listen to background sounds. Write for a couple of minutes.

GOAL MAP WITH BRIDGING

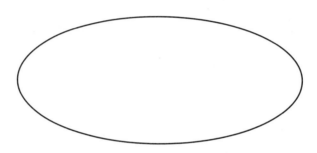

In this mind-body state, how are you more able to accomplish your goal?

_____

_____

Look at the thoughts on your map. Do any of them cause mental pressure and body tension? The thoughts that come without excess body tension and mental pressure indicate executive functioning and the presence of your powerful self.

Both maps you just did had the same self-improvement goal. In the first map you saw how your I-System's fixer adds stress, mind clutter, and body tension, making it difficult to achieve your goal. In the second map you quieted your I-System with your bridging awareness tools and shifted into executive functioning. You saw that when your I-System is at rest, your path to achieve your goal is clearer, your mind and body calm and relaxed. In this state, your powerful self in the executive mode is in control. Achieving your goal is now more possible and more fulfilling.

UNMASKING YOUR FIXER

Your days are filled with activities. Many of them may be free of stress (for example, brushing your teeth, playing with your dog, and receiving recognition for a job well done). Others (for example, rushing to an appointment or meeting, pushing yourself to meet a deadline, dealing with a never-ending list of demands for your time) could well be associated with body tension and urgent self-talk (storylines). Unmasking the fixer allows you to turn tension-filled activities into activities done with a resting I-System.

Think back over the past twenty-four hours and notice any specific body tension, mental pressure, or feelings of being driven. That's your fixer in action. See if you can find the different characteristics of body tension (location, type, or both) that come with your fixer.

Activity	Body Tension and Location	Storyline	Fixer Driven Thought
Rushing to an appointment	Tense neck, chest pressure	I can't be late again. Next time I'll start earlier!	Drive fast and go through yellow lights.

The fixer may also be involved when you can't seem to resolve an issue. Maybe at night when you're trying to sleep, a situation plays over and over in your mind. Your I-System's fixer is in high gear, trying to figure out how to fix everything, yet interfering with your sleep. Remember to use bridging awareness practices and thought labeling for a good night's sleep. A two-part What's on My Mind map before bed is very helpful. Quality sleep is your number one revitalizer.

DEFUSING YOUR FIXER IN YOUR ACTIVITIES

Mari, the harried mother mentioned earlier in this chapter, had trouble telling the difference between fixer thoughts and those from natural executive functioning until she began using her bridging awareness practices throughout the day. Now she comes out of her morning shower with a relatively calm mind and body. When she looks at the clock, thinks *The kids will be late for school*, and feels her shoulders tighten, she knows that her usual response—yelling, "You'll be late for school! Hurry up!"—comes from her fixer. She listens to the traffic sounds outside the window, feels her feet as she walks across the hall, feels her shoulders drop, and calmly gathers everyone up. She defuses her fixer and returns to executive functioning.

In the heat of any situation, you too can convert the fixer into natural executive functioning. Remember, the only time to defuse and stop your fixer is *during* an activity. Use your fixer recognition tools for several days and then fill out the below chart.

Activity	Telltale Signs of Your Fixer	Stress Reduction and Power Building Tools You Used	Results
Getting the kids ready for school	*Breathing faster, shoulders pulled up, do-or-die sense of urgency*	*Listened to background sounds, stayed aware of my body*	*Calmly got kids ready for school*
Worrying constantly about the IRS lien	*Chest pressure*	*Recognized my fixer*	*Carried on with my day without the 100-pound load on my back*

The fixer is so persistent in our lives that most of us come to see its activity as "It's just me." How many times have you ignored your body tension and dismissed your mind clutter with an "It's just me" attitude? Remember, when your I-System is active, you can defuse your fixer by simply being aware of its activity, using your bridging awareness tools, and then bringing your awareness back to what you were doing. Your challenge is to tell the difference between fixer and natural executive functioning. To do so it's helpful to have a strong daily bridging awareness practice. Then as soon as you begin to experience body tension, storylines, mental pressure, and feelings of being overwhelmed, you know it's the fixer. The release of the physical and mental tension signals that you have returned to your powerful self in the executive mode.

GIVING UP YOUR FIXER

1. Many people believe that their success in life is due solely to the drive and pressure of the fixer and even say, "If it wasn't for all this tension, I would have never accomplished anything." Do a map titled "What Will Happen to Me If I Give Up My Fixer?" Jot down whatever comes to mind when you imagine giving up your fixer (for example, *I won't have any motivation, I'll lose my job, I'll never accomplish anything, I won't be successful,* or *I'll never get well*). Write for a couple of minutes. Describe your body tension at the bottom of the map.

WHAT WILL HAPPEN IF
I GIVE UP MY FIXER?

Body Tension: _____

A. Is your mind cluttered or clear?

_____

B. Is your body tense or relaxed?

_____

C. Look at your map and list some of your requirements:

_____

_____

D. In this mind-body state, how do you act?

_____

Some people panic when doing this map. They feel as if they'll lose everything if they give up their fixers. People think, *To give up my fixer would be like giving up my right arm*! and *If I let my fixer go, I'll go right down the tubes.* They fear that if they relax, they'll be nothing, and they will fail. This reliance on the fixer is the I-System's empty promise, a promise that will never be fulfilled. The next map will demonstrate that when you quiet your I-System, you free yourself from the tyranny of your fixer and experience your limitless powerful self.

2. Do the previous map again, this time using your bridging awareness practices. Before you start writing, listen to background sounds, feel your body's pressure on your seat, sense your feet on the floor, and feel the pen in your hand. Take your time. Once you're settled, keep feeling the pen in your hand, and start writing. Watch the ink go onto the paper, and listen to background sounds. Write for a couple of minutes.

WHAT WILL HAPPEN IF I GIVE UP MY FIXER? MAP WITH BRIDGING

WHAT WILL HAPPEN IF
I GIVE UP MY FIXER?

A. Do you really need your fixer? Yes _____ No _____

B. Are you ready to let go of your fixer? Yes _____ No _____

C. With your executive functioning instead of the I-System's distortion, do you feel that you are not broken and don't need fixing? Yes _____ No _____

With a resting I-System, your powerful self functions naturally. In this unified, harmonious mind-body state, you access your power of healing, goodness, and wisdom and express that power by taking care of yourself and your responsibilities.

THE DANCE OF THE DEPRESSOR/FIXER

Not only does the depressor/fixer cycle cause sleepless nights, addictions, burnout, and impaired performance, it corrupts your important relationships, causing an enormous drain on your physical and mental resources. Recognition of your depressor/fixer cycle changes stress into power. Here are three guidelines for improving your relationships.

1. Even though your kids are having a difficult time and are hurting emotionally, they are not broken and don't need you to fix them. When you *recognize* that your depressor thoughts (*I'm not a good parent because they are hurting*) are driving your fixer activity (I need to make them feel better), your suffering and stress level will automatically decrease so you can be totally there for them with your expanded capacity and capabilities. You will be parenting your children with a resting I-System and full access to your wellspring of healing, goodness, and wisdom.

2. Even though a fellow worker, friend, or family member is currently having "tough times," you can't fix him, and your I-System's driven fixer activity can only make him feel damaged. When you use your bridging awareness practices and recognize your fixer, your caring and compassion can flow freely.

3. Your most important relationships involve combinations of natural executive functioning and I-System functioning. Recognizing your tendency to be driven by your depressor or fixer in relationships is helpful. For example, when you're depressed, sad, and frustrated, are you looking for your important others to fix you? If so, you are giving away your self-power while trying to take theirs. When you recognize and defuse your depressor, your relationship grows without the I-System's interference.

DON'T LET YOUR FIXER FOOL YOU

The I-System is not a static system; it may try to fool you by creating more fixers. For your continued progress, it's important to recognize new fixers as they come up. Some examples are:

- *I'm doing better, so I can relax and not do as much bridging.*

- *I'm good enough that I can do the maps in my head.*

- *It's okay to explode once in a while if the situation warrants it.*

- *I only need to bridge when I'm tense.*

- *If it feels good, I should do it, because it must be executive functioning.*

- *Bridging means having free choice, so any time I choose high-risk activities, it's okay.*

- *Natural executive functioning is always effortless, so I don't need to practice anymore.*

These fixers parade themselves as choices that come from natural executive functioning. But they have the same distinctive signs you learned earlier in this chapter (body tension, mental pressure, urgent storylines, and lack of clarity about the effect of your actions). What *is* new is that they present themselves in a way that makes you feel good about them, and you fail to recognize the elevated level of tension that is driving the choice. The fixer takes the path of least resistance. By recognizing the fixer and reducing your tension with your bridging awareness practices, your powerful self makes the choice, free of the I-System's influence.

WHO IS DOING IT?

"What should I do?" is a frequently asked question when a problem comes up. That's not the right question. The real question is not *what* should you do, but *who* is doing it: your powerless or powerful self? If your I-System is overactive and your powerless self is in charge, then nothing you do will ever be good enough. When your I-System rests, your naturally functioning powerful self is in the driver's seat taking the best action to solve the problem.

During the day, ask yourself *who* is doing the activity (walking, parenting, using the computer, paying bills, working, playing, and so forth). Is it your stress-filled self, driven by an overactive I-System, or is it your powerful self? Remember, it's not the activity but who's doing it that matters. The fixer can't *make* you powerful. Your self-power is always present when your I-System is resting and you are functioning in the executive mode. Awareness of who's doing it helps you shift from the powerless to the powerful self. Try it.

Describe what happened:

_____

_____

_____

PUTTING IT ALL TOGETHER

Ted was irritable most of the time. Even little things set him off. Prone to road rage, he often had to restrain himself from hurting others. For example, whenever someone drove too slowly, his neck bulged, his face reddened, and his head throbbed. Ted thought, *A guy driving twenty-five miles per hour in a forty-five-mile zone should be shot!* He started using bridging awareness practices and thought labeling as effective tools to "cool down." Continuing his practices, he came to see that his multiple requirements—*The mail should be on time, I should not be put on hold, Others shouldn't speak disrespectfully about my team*—had frequently created meltdowns that caused him many problems. As he came to realize that his anger was an attempt to fix himself and the world, his disposition changed. In fact, one time Ted and his wife were in the car rushing to deal with a family emergency when they came upon a stopped car blocking an intersection. Ted's wife told him to "get that guy moving." Ted got out of the car and, instead of getting angry, simply "saw an old guy who was lost, spent a few minutes calmly reassuring him by giving him directions, and then got back into the car." He then told us, "I had no idea I had that kindness in me."

Stress Reduction and Power Building Tools

➤ *Defusing the fixer*

➤ *Recognizing the depressor/fixer cycle*

➤ *Converting fixer activity into executive functioning*

MBB EVALUATION SCALE
REACH YOUR GOALS WITHOUT STRESS

Date: _____

After using the tools in this chapter for several days, check the description that best matches your practice for each question: hardly ever, occasionally, usually, almost always.

How often do you...	Hardly Ever	Occasionally	Usually	Almost Always
Notice the fixer's never-ending pressure and tension?				
Become aware of the body sensations associated with the fixer?				
Realize that the fixer can never fix the powerless self?				
Find the depressor embedded in the fixer?				
See the interplay of the fixer and the depressor?				
Recognize the storylines that came with the fixer?				
Change your behavior by recognizing the consequences of your fixer-driven activities?				
Notice the difference between fixer-driven activities and those from natural executive functioning?				
Recognize the fixer is not necessary for your success?				
Notice the release of tension and excess pressure when you defuse your fixer by using your stress reduction and power building tools?				
Function better at home and at work?				

List behaviors the fixer causes:

_____

_____

How did your behavior change when you recognized your fixer and shifted into executive functioning?

_____

_____

MBB SELF-POWER INDICATOR

Date: _____

This indicator should only be completed when you have integrated the stress reduction and power building tools from the first four chapters into your life. It allows you to objectively note your progress and systematically keep track of your life-changing experiences.

Over the past seven days, how did you do in these areas?

Circle the number under your answer.	Not at all	Several days	More than half the days	Nearly every day
1. I've had positive interest and pleasure in my activities.	0	1	3	5
2. I've felt optimistic, excited, and hopeful.	0	1	3	5
3. I've slept well and woken up feeling refreshed.	0	1	3	5
4. I've had lots of energy.	0	1	3	5
5. I've been able to focus on tasks and use self-discipline.	0	1	3	5
6. I've stayed healthy, eaten well, exercised, and had fun.	0	1	3	5
7. I've felt good about my relationships with my family and friends.	0	1	3	5
8. I've been satisfied with my accomplishments at home, work, or school.	0	1	3	5
9. I've been comfortable with my financial situation.	0	1	3	5
10. I've felt good about the spiritual base of my life.	0	1	3	5
11. I've been satisfied with the direction of my life.	0	1	3	5
12. I've felt fulfilled, with a sense of well-being and peace of mind.	0	1	3	5

Score Key: Column Total   ____   ____   ____   ____

0-15 . . . . .Poor Self-Power

16-30 . . . . Fair Self-Power   Total Score _____

31-45 . . . . .Good Self-Power

46 and above . . . . Excellent Self-Power

CHAPTER 5

CONVERT STRESS INTO SELF-POWER BY MANAGING REQUIREMENTS

Principle: Requirements cause stress when they are not defused.

Principle: Defusing requirements immediately prevents stress and builds self-power.

Mind-Body Language:

Defusing requirements: When using all your stress reduction and power building tools, you handle a situation that previously activated your I-System with a stress-free, ready, and relaxed mind and body. Even when the picture of how you and the world should be is not fulfilled, the requirement is powerless to activate your I-System.

YOUR ON/OFF STRESS SWITCH

Let's summarize what you learned in the previous chapters. The I-System, like a light switch, is a stress switch that can be on or off. The natural state of the I-System is off. When it's off, you have a calm body, a clear mind, and a reservoir of self-power. It's only turned on by requirements. You control the on/off switch by recognizing and defusing your requirements.

The diagram in figure 5.1 demonstrates how your mind works. All thoughts naturally flow into the lower, executive functioning loop when your I-System is switched off. In this unified mind-body state you experience harmony and balance, and you live your best life. This lower loop is your birthright; it's always with you, optimizing your self-power. For example, when you are in the executive functioning loop and you face a new stressful situation (stressor), it does not lead to inner stress; it leads to your ever-improving ability to deal with your constantly changing reality. Contrast this to facing a new stressful situation (stressor) when you are in the I-System loop. Here your learning, coping, and problem-solving skills are impaired, resulting in stress overload and powerlessness.

When you are in the executive functioning loop you convert stressful situations into opportunities, which allows your self-power to grow no matter what life throws at you. Thus, rather than causing mind-body dysfunction, the stressors become merely situations where your powerful self is in control.

In this chapter, you will map requirements you have for yourself, others, and situations. Don't let your I-System fool you into thinking you can do maps in your head. When you put your thoughts on paper and recognize your body sensations, a powerful mind-body free-association process takes place. The unexpected thought is often the underlying requirement. This is where your "aha" moments can happen. Each map is placed strategically to maximize your insights into each situation and to put you in the executive mode. The more you are in the executive functioning loop, the quicker and easier it'll be to recognize and defuse your requirements as they arise in your life. Recognizing a requirement means that whenever you are distressed, you are able to identify the mental rule that has been broken about how you and the world should be. Defusing a requirement means that you are now able to face that same situation that previously caused distress and meltdown with a ready, relaxed mind and body. No matter what the situation is, defusing requirements keeps your stress switched off. Consistently using your stress reduction and power building tools means you'll live more and more of your life in the stress-free executive functioning loop.

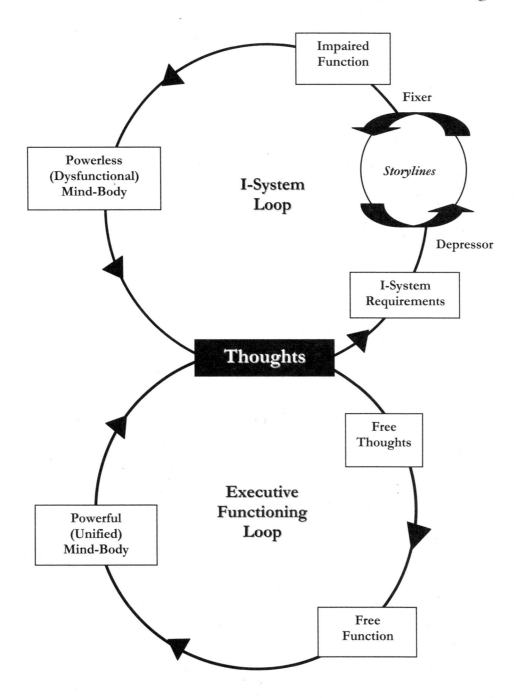

Figure 5.1: The I-System Loop and the Executive Functioning Loop

The mind works with thoughts. They naturally flow into the executive functioning loop, where you effectively take care of yourself and your responsibilities without stress overload. With a resting I-System, you naturally think, perceive the world, and act with free thoughts and free function. When your thoughts become requirements for yourself and the world, you are pulled up into the I-System loop, where the mind-body commotion of the I-System creates an unsatisfying and stress-filled life.

KEEPING YOUR STRESS SWITCH OFF IN A DISTRESSING EXPERIENCE

1. We have all had days when someone's inappropriate behavior has caused us a great deal of distress. Map the most distressing recent experience caused by another person's behavior. Write the behavior at the top of the map (*My boss lied to me*), and write how you wanted that person to act (*My boss shouldn't lie* or *My boss should tell the truth*) in the center of the oval. Take a couple of minutes to scatter your thoughts around the oval as you think about that person's behavior. Describe your body tension at the bottom of the map.

DISTRESSING EXPERIENCE MAP

Other Person's Behavior: _____

Body Tension: _____

A. Is your mind cluttered? Yes _____ No _____

B. Is your distress due to the other person's behavior? Yes _____ No _____

C. Is the distress due to the requirement in the oval? Yes _____ No _____

If you believe the distress was from the other person's behavior, you are letting yourself be victimized by circumstances. As long as you do not recognize that how you wanted the other person to act is *your* requirement, you will suffer distress and stay in the I-System loop. Recognizing your requirement and seeing what that requirement is doing to you prompts a dramatic mental and physical shift so that you are no longer a victim of circumstance.

2. Write the same behavior on the following line, and in the oval, write how you wanted the other person to act. Before you continue writing, listen to background sounds, feel your body's pressure on your seat, sense your feet on the floor, and feel the pen in your hand. Take your time. Once you feel settled, keep feeling the pen in your hand and start writing. Watch the ink go onto the paper and listen to background sounds. Write for a couple of minutes.

DISTRESSING EXPERIENCE MAP WITH BRIDGING

Other Person's Behavior: _____

A. How is this map the same as or different from the previous map?

_____

_____

B. Are you a victim of circumstance? Yes _____ No _____

C. Is your stress switched off? Yes _____ No _____

Do you see how, on the first map in this exercise, the statement in the oval was a requirement because it activated your I-System? On this map, after using your bridging awareness tools to quiet your I-System, the same statement in the oval was *no longer* a requirement. It became a natural thought or expectation because your I-System was calm and your body tension and mind clutter were dramatically reduced. You are now prepared to deal with that same situation with a clear mind and relaxed body. Your mind-body bridging practice doesn't take away your natural expectations of how others should behave, but it does take away the devastation your requirements cause. Using your stress reduction and power building tools (especially mapping) prepares you to deal actively and confidently with your life circumstances.

FINDING REQUIREMENTS THAT CAUSE YOUR DISTRESS

Tori was a high-powered, successful twenty-eight-year-old executive. She and her husband Scott agreed that he would be the stay-at-home parent, taking care of their children and the household responsibilities. This arrangement seemed to be working, but Tori was becoming more and more critical and irritated with Scott. She described not having dinner on the table when she came home, toys not being put away, and Scott's forgetting to pick up her clothes at the cleaners. No matter how hard Scott tried, it seemed he always missed something. Tori said, "I almost didn't want to come home because it made me feel angry and miserable." She learned about mind-body bridging and took to mapping like a fish to water. Tori did a series of maps that totally changed her life. The first was a "Requirement for Scott" map. It was filled with *Scott should do this, should do that, should do....* When she did the last map in the series, it was a "What Would It Look Like if Scott Fulfilled All My Requirements" map. After completing that map, she broke out sobbing and then couldn't stop herself from laughing. She had again written *he should do this, and that, and do...*, but she finally wrote *He would be my slave.* Sobbing, she concluded, "I'm trying to make myself a slave master, which I totally despise when men do it." Tori continued to integrate mind-body bridging practices into her everyday life and climb the corporate ladder, and her coming home after work became a "true joy that I look forward to. Scott and I are closer than ever before."

List the situations from the past few days that prompted you to become upset, tense, irritable, anxious, or overwhelmed. Realize that it's always the underlying requirement that you weren't yet aware of, and not the event, that's causing your distress. Recognizing your underlying requirement prompts changes in your thoughts and actions.

Situation	How You Handled the Situation	Unfulfilled Requirement
My spouse said I'll never change.	*I yelled "Go to hell" and didn't talk to him all day.*	*My spouse should accept me as I am.*
I couldn't find my car keys.	*I looked everywhere for them and became angry and frustrated.*	*I should always know where I put my car keys.*

HANDLING YOUR NEMESIS WITH YOUR STRESS SWITCH OFF

1. Do a My Nemesis map. Pick the person who has been causing you the most grief and write his or her name in the oval. Take a couple of minutes to jot whatever thoughts come to mind. Describe your body tension at the bottom of the map.

MY NEMESIS MAP

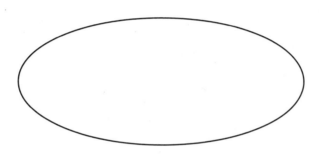

Body Tension: _____

A. Do you think your nemesis is causing your mind-body distress? Yes _____ No _____

B. Identify the requirements on your map (for example, *She shouldn't bully me, He shouldn't talk down to me, He shouldn't stab me in the back, She shouldn't talk about me*):

_____

_____

_____

Your I-System's commotion machine has you feeling distressed, bitter, angry, and hopeless and believing that anyone in your shoes would feel the same way. Now ask yourself, *Isn't it bad enough that they act that way? Why do I have to let my I-System cause me a personal meltdown, limiting my ability to deal with this person and the situation?* Remember, you have no control over others' behavior. You do have control over defusing your requirements and reducing your stress in troubling relationships or situations.

2. Do this map using your bridging awareness practices. Write that same person's name in the oval. Before you continue writing, listen to any background sounds; feel your body's pressure on your seat, sense your feet on the floor, and feel the pen in your hand. Take your time. Once you feel settled, keep feeling the pen in your hand, and start writing. Watch the ink go onto the paper, and listen to any background sounds. For the next few minutes, jot down whatever thoughts pop into your mind.

MY NEMESIS MAP WITH BRIDGING

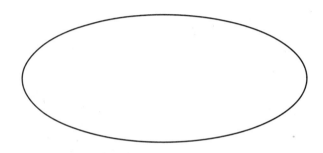

A. How did your mind-body state differ between the two maps?

_____

_____

B. Can you see that it's your I-System, not the nemesis, that's causing your distress?

_____

C. Which mind-body state lets you deal most effectively with your nemesis?

_____

You now know firsthand that it's your I-System, not the nemesis, causing your stress and misery, keeping you from your powerful self. Also, this activity shows the power of a strong daily bridging awareness practice. When you feel body tension, use your bridging awareness tools to create the emotional space you need to defuse requirements and deal with difficult situations during your busy day.

LOOKING BACK AT A VERY STRESSFUL DAY

1. Think about the most stressful day you've had in the last several weeks.

A. What were your stressors that day?

_____

_____

B. How active was your depressor?

_____

_____

C. How did your fixer respond?

_____

_____

D. Did your storylines keep the depressor/fixer going? Yes _____ No _____

E. List the requirements you had for yourself and the situation:

_____

_____

F. How did you handle that day? Was your I-System or your powerful self in control?

_____

Beata and Maciej were engaged and looking forward to being married in Warsaw. Beata was the daughter of very old-fashioned university professors who didn't like that Maciej was older than their daughter. They resented the fact that Maciej was less educated than Beata and was earning substantially less money than she was. Maciej would develop severe stress symptoms three days before Beata's parents visited and remain tense and withdrawn throughout their visit.

After finding and working with an online mind-body bridging coach, Maciej began mapping. After doing a two-part Stressor map, he became silent for several minutes. The coach started thinking that the online link had been dropped until Maciej's voice came over the headphones, and said "I can't see." The coach inquired, "What can't you see?" Maciej responded, "I cannot see the problem anymore. It evaporated."

Maciej's quiet voice contained a note of excitement and sincere surprise. He had realized that his major requirement was to be liked by Beata's parents. He reported to his coach several weeks later that Beata's parent's visits didn't stress him out anymore. He even started enjoying them.

2. Use your bridging awareness practices and do a map about that same stressful day. Before you start writing, listen to any background sounds; feel your body's pressure on your seat, sense your feet on the floor, and feel the pen in your hand. Take your time. Once you feel settled, keep feeling the pen in your hand, and start writing. Watch the ink go onto the paper, and listen to any background sounds. For the next few minutes, jot down whatever thoughts pop into your mind.

| STRESSFUL DAY MAP WITH BRIDGING |

MOST STRESSFUL DAY

A. Is your mind cluttered or clear?

_____

B. Is your body tense or relaxed?

_____

C. Are you beginning to understand that your I-System, and not the stressors in your day, causes you distress? Yes _____ No _____

Your stress reduction and power building tools help you deal with any stressors that can come up in your life.

MY PERFECT WORLD: POSSIBLE OR IMPOSSIBLE?

Do a How My World Would Look If My Requirements for Others Were Met map. Scatter your thoughts around the oval for a couple of minutes. Be as specific as you can (for example, *My spouse would always take care of me, Jason would not be a jerk, My neighbor would mind his own business, My coworkers would do their jobs*).

HOW MY WORLD WOULD LOOK IF MY REQUIREMENTS FOR OTHERS WERE MET

Observations:

_____

_____

_____

_____

_____

Even if your partner, boss, friend, or neighbor met all your requirements, your I-System would always create more requirements. Defusing requirements is a skill that will help you throughout your life.

RECOGNIZE AND DEFUSE REQUIREMENTS TO GAIN CONTROL OF YOUR STRESS

Becoming distressed and overwhelmed means you have a requirement you aren't yet aware of. Use these steps to help you recognize and defuse your requirements:

1. Become aware of the earliest signs of an overactive I-System (such as noticing specific body tension, as well as depressor, fixer, and storyline activity), and let them prompt you to look for the underlying requirement.

2. Practice your recognizing and defusing requirement skills by using them in simple situations—such as waiting for a long red light, experiencing a dropped phone call, or dealing with impolite clerks—and gradually build to using your skills in more complex relationships and situations.

3. Use your bridging awareness practice and thought labeling tools to interrupt the I-System's commotion machine and then identify the underlying requirement. Remind yourself that it's *your* requirement about the activity, person, or situation—*not* the activity, person, or situation—that's causing your distress.

4. Once you feel a release (gradual or sudden) about the situation, you have defused your requirement. That previously out-of-control devastation melts into a more manageable disappointment.

Describe what happened when you used your stress reduction and power building tools to defuse your requirements in a meltdown situation. Here's an example someone shared with us:

"Recently, I learned that my twelve-year-old son was smoking. I became enraged, screaming at him and threatening him, which gave me a migraine. Later, when I found out he was smoking again, I felt my jaw tighten. Noticing this signal, I realized my I-System was switched on. I then listened to the sound of the dogs barking outside, which made me feel more settled and helped me see my requirement: *My twelve-year-old son shouldn't smoke.* I was now clear that it was my requirement, not his behavior, that caused my *added* distress. I was really disappointed in my son but didn't melt down. I was able to calm myself down enough to discuss the situation with my son, and we were able to decide on a course of action."

_____

_____

_____

_____

When you quiet your I-System and defuse your requirements, you are in the executive functioning loop (figure 5.1), where your powerful self is in charge. Not only does your body settle and your thinking become clearer; your choices come naturally.

DIFFICULT-TO-DEFUSE REQUIREMENTS

Your I-System has been very busy defining how you and your world should be. Some requirements are easy to defuse, while others haven't budged. For the more difficult-to-defuse requirements, it helps to first focus on the behavior that triggered your requirement and then break that behavior down into smaller parts. For example, rather than deal with a general behavior like *My boss doesn't appreciate me*, break it down into many smaller, specific behaviors: *the way he looks at me, the way he smiles at others, the critical tone of his voice, the sharp words he uses.* This allows you to recognize very specific requirements: *He should look at me kindly, He should smile at me, He should speak in a supportive voice,* and *He should use gentle words.* Next, use your bridging awareness practices on each of these separate requirements. Remember, after you recognize a requirement, it's ready to be defused.

Over the next few days, recognize and defuse your requirements as they come up.

1. Describe which stress reduction and power building tools worked:

_____

_____

2. List the requirements you were able to defuse and those you were *not* able to defuse:

Was Able to Defuse	Could Not Defuse
My husband should have dinner ready on time. *My husband should pick up his towel.*	*My brother-in-law should get out of our lives.* *My son should do his homework.*

In dealing with a requirement like *My son should do his homework,* your I-System would have you believe that you are a bad parent because he doesn't do his homework. Remember, the goal of mind-body bridging is not to get your son to do his homework, but to defuse your requirement about his doing his homework. Then you shift into your executive mode and have the resources to relate to your son differently.

3. From the previous chart, choose the requirement that has been the most difficult to defuse. Write it in the oval. Next, scatter your thoughts around the oval for a couple of minutes without editing them. Describe your body tension at the bottom of the map.

MOST DIFFICULT TO DEFUSE REQUIREMENT MAP

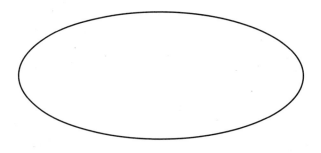

Body Tension: _____

What's your overactive I-System doing?

A. What are your depressors?

_____

B. What are your fixers?

_____

C. What are your storylines?

_____

D. What are your additional requirements?

_____

_____

4. Do this map again, using your bridging awareness practices. Write the same requirement in the oval. Before you start writing, listen to any background sounds; feel your body's pressure on your seat, sense your feet on the floor, and feel the pen in your hand. Take your time. Once you feel settled, keep feeling the pen in your hand, and start writing. Watch the ink go onto the paper, and listen to any background sounds. For the next few minutes, jot down whatever thoughts pop into your mind.

MOST DIFFICULT TO DEFUSE REQUIREMENT MAP
WITH BRIDGING

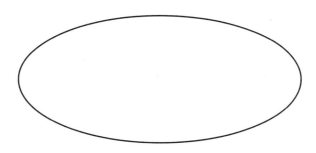

A. How is this map the same as or different from the previous map?

_____

_____

B. How would you act in the same situation with a quiet I-System?

_____

_____

It's important to use your stress reduction and power building tools to defuse your requirements when the situation comes up again.

LETTING GO OF YOUR REQUIREMENTS

1. Do a What Will Happen If I Let Go of All My Requirements for the World map. Scatter your thoughts around the oval for several minutes.

```
        WHAT WILL
   HAPPEN IF I LET GO OF
   ALL MY REQUIREMENTS
      FOR THE WORLD
```

A. Does your I-System's commotion machine leave you feeling weak and fearful and believing you will lose control of your life? Yes _____ No _____

B. Write your level of body tension by each item on the map, using Ø for none, + for minimal, ++ for moderate, or +++ for severe. See the sample map that follows. Next list below those items that come with body tension and identify their underlying requirements:

Item with Body Tension	Requirement

SAMPLE MAP: WHAT WILL HAPPEN IF I LET GO OF ALL MY REQUIREMENTS FOR THE WORLD

No one will get any-
thing done +++

Nothing will be
done right +++

People will take
advantage of me +++

WHAT WILL
HAPPEN IF I LET GO OF
ALL MY REQUIREMENTS
FOR THE WORLD

Things will go
smoother Ø

My partner will see
me as weak +++

Len will spend too
much time with his
friends ++

Item with Body Tension	Requirement
My partner will see me as weak.	*My partner should see me as strong.*
Len will spend too much time with his friends.	*Len should spend less time with his friends.*
People will take advantage of me.	*People shouldn't take advantage of me.*

2. Do the map again, this time using your bridging awareness practices. Before you start writing, listen to background sounds, feel your body's pressure on your seat, sense your feet on the floor, and feel the pen in your hand. Take your time. Once you're settled, keep feeling the pen in your hand, and start writing your thoughts. Watch the ink go onto the paper, and listen to background sounds. Write for a couple of minutes.

> ## WHAT WILL HAPPEN IF I LET GO OF ALL MY REQUIREMENTS FOR THE WORLD MAP WITH BRIDGING

WHAT WILL
HAPPEN IF I LET GO OF
ALL MY REQUIREMENTS
FOR THE WORLD

What are the differences between the two maps?

_____

_____

_____

_____

Is it becoming clearer that having I-System requirements is destructive to you and your world? Requirements restrict your ability to deal effectively with other people and situations. When you rest your I-System, your powerful self can respond actively, attentively, and assertively in your relationships and situations. You'll be able to face each moment while having full access to your inner wellspring of healing, goodness, and wisdom. Your powerful self is in charge.

PUTTING IT ALL TOGETHER

A government worker was continually frustrated by the slow pace and "marginal" performance of the staff he supervised. He followed the manual for his position and even talked with his supervisor, all to no avail. His job wasn't in jeopardy, but his job satisfaction was at an all-time low. "I was getting burned out. I did all I could and they didn't budge," he said. One worker even told him, "We're following our job descriptions and there is nothing you can do." His wife suggested mind-body bridging because it had improved her life. At first he resisted, saying it was "just the way it is and nothing can change. Quitting is the only solution to my problems and I can't quit because I have twenty-three years with the government." His anger over the situation was communicated to everyone in his tone of voice, posture, and demeanor. After giving mind-body bridging a try, he realized that his requirements for the people he supervised were pushing him to "fix" them. When he used his bridging awareness practices, thought labeling, and mapping, his life at home and work changed. He recognized it was *his* requirements (*They should work as hard as I do, They should be more productive, They shouldn't take such long breaks*) that were causing all his stress. "I realized that I was not powerless because they didn't work hard, they weren't broken because they weren't more productive, and I didn't need to fix them or myself." He saw an automatic shift in himself. He became open to interacting with his staff, and his division's productivity increased while their sick days decreased.

Defusing requirements is a very important stress reduction and power building tool. Remember, it takes all of your tools to become proficient in switching off your I-System. Turning off your stress switch automatically gives you access to your executive functioning self-power. The remainder of this book is a guide to help you defuse requirements in every aspect of your life.

Stress Reduction and Power Building Tool

➤ *Defusing requirements for others and for situations*

MBB EVALUATION SCALE
CONVERT STRESS INTO SELF-POWER
BY MANAGING REQUIREMENTS

Date: _____

After using the tool in this chapter for several days, check the description that best matches your practice for each question: hardly ever, occasionally, usually, almost always.

How often do you...	Hardly Ever	Occasionally	Usually	Almost Always
Recognize that requirements always trigger your I-System and impair your functioning?				
Recognize that requirements that you are not aware of are responsible for your daily stress?				
Prevent stress by defusing a requirement?				
See that requirements you have for others or situations are trapping you, preventing you from becoming who you really are?				
Interrupt storylines by using thought labeling and bridging awareness practices?				
Recognize the powerless self?				
Experience the powerless self as a myth of the I-System?				
Experience your powerful self when your I-System is switched off?				
Know it's your powerful self when you are naturally functioning moment by moment (executive functioning loop)?				
Come to appreciate aspects of your everyday life?				
Experience connection to a wellspring of healing, goodness, and wisdom?				
Find that your relationships have improved?				
Function better at home and at work?				

List three requirements you defused that had previously caused meltdowns. How did you deal with each situation in the executive functioning loop?

1. _____

2. _____

3. _____

CHAPTER 6

BUILD A STRESS-FREE FOUNDATION FOR YOUR RELATIONSHIPS

Principle: An overactive I-System negatively impacts your relationships.

Principle: A resting I-System empowers your relationships.

RELATIONSHIPS AND YOUR I-SYSTEM

Your I-System's requirements get you into relationships you shouldn't be in, keep you out of relationships that are mutually beneficial, and most important, create stress in your present relationships.

A counselor told us that he had a client whose partner simply "did not leave me alone." Her partner would call her many times at night, and if she didn't answer, he would start calling her place of work, putting her job in jeopardy. She felt she couldn't warn her employer because it would result in a loss of face. In her non-Western culture, taking the legal step of filing a complaint for stalking was out of the question. She felt she no longer had a life of her own. She felt exhausted, depressed, powerless, and stressed "to the point of breaking." She reported sleeplessness, continuous "heartache and palpitations," and general health issues.

She began a mind-body bridging program to reduce her stress. Soon the simple act of tuning in to background sounds or concentrating on the vibrations of public transport began quieting her I-System, allowing her time away from her depressor/fixer's spinning thoughts and a tension-filled body. She was progressively able to incorporate the sound of the phone ringing into her bridging awareness practice. Her "aha" moments occurred while she was mapping. She learned about her triggers (*her partner's persistent calls, his endless demands on her time*) and mapped her I-System's requirements (*he shouldn't call me all the time, he shouldn't be so demanding*) for her relationship. By continuing to map, she recognized the underlying requirement for herself (*I should please my partner*). This recognition moved her from a state of powerlessness and despondency to executive functioning, where she could find solutions to address her relationship, free of her I-System. She reported that her stress levels dropped significantly, and her ability to make choices increased. She established more appropriate boundaries for her relationship and had more energy to focus on her life.

It's important to remember that defusing requirements like *He shouldn't be so demanding, He should respect me,* or *I should please my partner* doesn't mean you give up your natural expectations of acceptable behavior for your partner and yourself. What it does mean is that when your partner's behavior violates a defused requirement (your natural expectation), you have the ability to respond appropriately, actively, and assertively to the situation. If that requirement were not defused, your ability to respond would be limited by your activated I-System.

The requirements you have for yourself are constantly creating stress, interfering with your relationships, impairing your quality of life, and preventing you from being who you are meant to be. You know how painful it is when others don't accept who you are. But what about the pain you put yourself through when you don't accept yourself? Can you imagine the relief when your inner critic is quiet, allowing your executive functioning to be in the driver's seat? When you defuse the unremitting self-demands (requirements for yourself), the foundations of your relationships are strengthened. The real stressor in your relationships is not the other person, not your limitations, but your overactive I-System.

BEING YOURSELF RIGHT HERE AND NOW

"Being in the moment" has become a popular theme in improving relationships. But the problem is not being in the moment, because there has never been a human being who isn't in the moment. You can only breathe now; you can only act now; your heart can't pump yesterday's blood or tomorrow's blood. It can only beat right here, right now. It's impossible to not live in the present moment. The problem is that the I-System, when activated by requirements, uproots us from experiencing and expressing the essence of who we are right here, right now. Let's see how it works.

Do a How I Want to Be map. *Inside* the circle, write how you would like to be right here, right now (for example, *organized, healthy, strong, calm, attractive*). Be specific! After you have listed at least six qualities, write the opposite of each quality *outside* the circle. Connect the quality inside the circle with a line to its opposite outside the circle. If needed, see the sample map that follows.

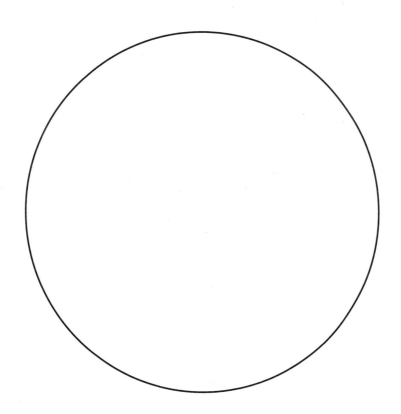

HOW I WANT TO BE RIGHT HERE, RIGHT NOW MAP

SAMPLE MAP: HOW I WANT TO BE RIGHT HERE, RIGHT NOW

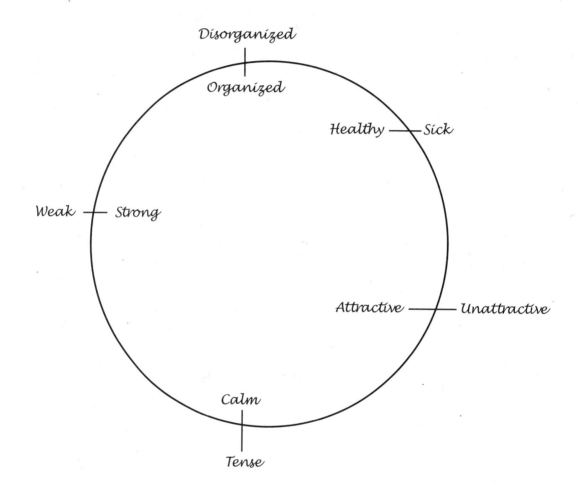

A. How do the qualities *inside* the circle make you feel?

_____

_____

_____

B. How do the qualities *outside* the circle make you feel?

_____

_____

_____

If the qualities *outside* the circle create body tension with a negative emotional response, they are triggers. Remember, a trigger (an event or thought) is a signal that a requirement has activated your I-System. This means that those opposite qualities (about how you want to be) *inside* the circle are requirements. Once your requirement is defused, the trigger no longer activates your I-System.

C. From your map, list your triggers and requirements about how you want to be:

Trigger	Requirement
Being disorganized	*I should be organized.*

D. Are you beginning to understand that when your natural expectation has been captured by your I-System and it becomes a requirement, your self-esteem suffers, and you will never be satisfied, because enough will never be enough? Yes _____ No _____

MIRROR, MIRROR ON THE WALL

How's your self-image? Do you really want to know? Are you ready to let it all hang out?

1. Let's do a Mirror map. Find a quiet place and look in a mirror. Before you start writing, really look at yourself for a minute or so. Next, scatter around the oval any thoughts and feelings that come to mind about what you see. Try not to censor anything. Glance back at the mirror several times and keep writing whatever comes to mind. Describe your body tension at the bottom of the map.

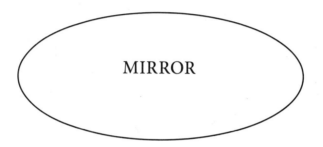

Body Tension: _____

A. Is your I-System active? Yes _____ No _____

B. Do you recognize your depressor? Yes _____ No _____

C. What are your storylines?

_____

_____

_____

D. Do you recognize that the depressor's activity is causing you to experience your face as an enemy and draining your self-power? Yes _____ No _____

E. What are your requirements?

_____

_____

2. Do another Mirror map, this time using your bridging awareness practices. Before writing, listen to any background sounds, feel your body's pressure on your seat, sense your feet on the floor, and feel the pen in your hand. Now look in the mirror and keep listening to background sounds. Take your time. After you feel settled, jot around the oval whatever thoughts pop into your mind. Keep listening to background sounds and feeling the pen in your hand. Watch the ink go onto the paper. Write for a couple of minutes.

MIRROR MAP WITH BRIDGING

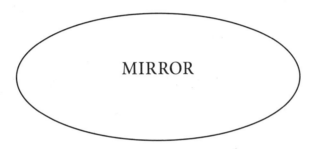

MIRROR

A. How is this map different from your first Mirror map?

_____

_____

B. Did the facial features you see in the mirror change? Yes _____ No _____

C. Using mind-body bridging awareness practices, do you have a new level of self-acceptance? Yes _____ No _____

Take a good look at your image in the mirror every morning and again at night. Let your thoughts flow freely, and monitor your body tension. Notice the telltale signs of your overactive I-System. Become aware of your depressor, your fixer, and, most important, your requirements for yourself. Over time observe how your self-image improves without your having to try to fix yourself. This shift in self-acceptance that comes with a continuing stress reduction and power building practice is an indicator of your increasing self-power. When you use your bridging awareness practices, the foundation of who you are is grounded in your powerful self.

KEEPING THE PAST IN THE PAST

Is your past restricting how you live your life, preventing you from being who you are meant to be right here, right now? Our past experiences can either positively or negatively impact our lives. The following maps will allow you to discover whether your past is a burden or a resource.

Do a How I Got to Be the Way I Am map. Around the oval, write how you got to be the way you are (for example, *My father was never around, I went through two unhappy marriages, Mom was always there to support me*). Write for a couple of minutes. Describe your body tension at the bottom of the map. A sample map follows.

```
            _____
         /                               \
        /                                 \
       /        HOW I GOT TO BE            \
       \        THE WAY I AM               /
        \                                 /
         \                               /
            _____
```

Body Tension: _____

A. What storyline themes run through your map?

_____

_____

B. Describe when and how often you use these storylines—for example, when you feel like a success or failure, when you're sad or happy, or when you're bored or busy:

_____

_____

The I-System uses stories (positive and negative, past and future) to keep you from living in the present. No matter what the content, storylines tense your body, limit your awareness, and impair your ability to function, strengthening your false belief in the powerless self. Being more aware of your storylines quiets your I-System so that you automatically start experiencing your powerful self right here, right now. When you are in the executive functioning loop and thoughts of the past arise, they are simply thoughts without the heat and spin of the I-System.

SAMPLE MAP: HOW I GOT TO BE THE WAY I AM

Poor school district

Mom was depressed

I always knew Mom
loved me, but she
didn't show it

Dad wasn't
around much

I learned a lot
from all the jobs
I've had

HOW I GOT TO BE
THE WAY I AM

One of my teachers
helped me feel good
about myself

I never gave up

I went to a great college

I was fine before
my parents divorced

My friends always
had my back

My most important
experience was learning
I was a survivor

Body Tension: *headache, stiff neck*

YOUR SELF-IMAGE: FRIEND OR FOE?

You don't have to get rid of your negative self-image. You don't have to generate a positive self-image either. When your I-System is resting, your powerful self will flow from every cell of your body.

A forty-five-year-old office worker and mother of two had a husband who informed her that he "found a better deal out there." Her self-image took a dive and she felt unlovable. As the divorce dragged on, she began looking for something to relieve her stress and found that tranquilizers had too many side effects. Her coworker suggested mind-body bridging to help with the stress in her life. She used her bridging awareness practices and thought labeling to settle herself down. Then she began mapping her divorce and her negative self-image. As she discovered her requirements (*I should look younger, I should have been all he needed, I should be loved for who I am*), she came to understand her depressor/fixer dance (*I'm too old so I'll get a face-lift and get in better shape because I'm not thin enough*). She was now able to defuse her requirements. Her crying, frustration, and anger ended. Her self-power allowed her to become assertive; she became an active participant in her divorce (no longer a victim of her powerless self), hammered out support for her children, and began a new relationship.

STRESS REDUCTION AND POWER BUILDING TOOLS FOR IMPROVING YOUR SELF-IMAGE

- *Bridging awareness practices*—When you notice negative self-talk and body tension in your life, recognize it as a sign of an overactive I-System, tune in to your senses, and then mindfully return to what you were doing.

- *Thought labeling*—When a negative thought pops into your mind, remember, a thought is just a thought. Label your negative thoughts as mere thoughts, and return to what you were doing. For example, when *I'll never be the same* pops into your mind, say to yourself, *I'm having the thought "I'll never be the same," and it's just a thought.*

- *Storyline awareness*—When you catch yourself mulling over stories about negative self-beliefs, notice the repetitive themes, recognize them as storylines, and return to the task at hand. It doesn't matter if the stories are true or false, positive or negative. Remember, it's not your negative thoughts that get you down or your positive thoughts that pull you up; your storylines create mind clutter and fill every cell of your body with tension, supporting the depressor-fixer dance. Your I-System capturing your stories is what takes you away from the present.

- *Mapping*—Use the two-part mind-body maps. The first map helps you find the requirements that reinforce your negative self-beliefs. Noticing your body tension is what helps you find these requirements. Use your bridging awareness practices on the second map to see the truth about negative self-beliefs and return to executive functioning.

- *Defusing requirements*—When you notice body tension and negative self-talk, quiet your I-System, and then identify your requirement (for example, if the negative self-talk is *I'm unlovable*, the requirement is *I should be loved*). Remember, your current distress is from an overactive I-System, not the situation or your negative thoughts. Being aware of your requirement as it comes up in real time reduces its power. You will know you have defused the requirement when you notice a sudden or gradual release of body tension and your mind clears.

POWERING YOUR SELF-IMAGE TRANSFORMS YOUR LIFE

Use your stress reduction and power building tools today to keep your negative self-image and self-talk from getting you down and interfering with your life, then fill out the chart below.

Negative Self-Image	Body Tension	What Stress Reduction Tools Did You Use and How	Body Sensations	How Your Behavior Changed After Using Your Tools
I'm not smart enough to get ahead in the world.	Chest tight, shallow breath	Labeled my thoughts Listened to hum of air conditioner	Chest and breathing relaxed	Wasn't as depressed Accomplished a lot on the job today
I'm unlovable	Gut cramps	I immediately recognized the thought "I should be lovable" as a requirement.	Calmer	"Light came on," day went smoothly Had a great time on my date

It's not your self-image that's interfering with your life; it's your I-System's requirements about your self-image that keep you from believing in who you are right here and now. When captured by your I-System, your self-image requirements disconnect you from your powerful self and from executive functioning. No matter who you are or what you have been through, your mind-body stress reduction and power building tools can change your life.

MEETING OR NOT MEETING REQUIREMENTS FOR YOURSELF

1. List three situations from the last several days where your requirements for yourself activated your I-System. For example, *I should know the answer when my boss asks me a question, I should be home on time, I shouldn't be alone, I shouldn't make a mistake.*

Situation	Requirement for Yourself
At our morning meeting, my boss asked me a question.	*I should know the answer when my boss asks me a question.*

2. Fill out this chart based on what you listed in the above chart:

Body Tension and Mind Clutter When Your Requirement Is Met	Body Tension and Mind Clutter When Your Requirement Is *Not* Met
Stomach tight, foot jiggles, hands grip chair arms tightly, have to just keep pushing	*Face hot, pressure in my chest, dry mouth, I'm stupid*

3. Fill out the next chart for each requirement from the previous chart:

Storylines When Meeting Requirement	Storylines When Not Meeting Requirement
I am so good, It's a relief, It's over, I'll know the answers for tomorrow's meeting	*I'll never have everything they want, It's my fault because I'm not good enough, It's always the same*

4. Fill out the next chart using the same requirements:

Your Behavior When Meeting Requirement	Your Behavior When Not Meeting Requirement
Puffed up and laughed too loud, interrupted my colleagues	*Shut down and stopped interacting with my colleagues*

The I-System has you between a rock and a hard place. When your requirements for yourself aren't met, your depressor moves into the driver's seat, leaving you powerless. Even when you are able to meet your requirements, the fixer moves into the driver's seat and enough is never enough. It's not a matter of fulfilling or not fulfilling your requirements, but one of defusing them. When your requirements are defused your powerful self is in the driver's seat, and you naturally take the right action moment by moment.

5. Using your bridging awareness practices, listen to background sounds, feel your body's pressure on your seat, sense your feet on the floor, and feel the pen in your hand. When you're settled, label your thoughts and go over each requirement you listed in the first chart in this exercise. What have you noticed about each of your requirements after mind-body bridging?

Requirement 1:

_____

Requirement 2:

_____

Requirement 3:

_____

YOUR EVERYDAY RELATIONSHIPS

Now that you know how critical a resting I-System is for your self-esteem, it's time to tackle your relationships. We all have natural aspirations and expectations for ourselves, our partners, and those with whom we have casual relationships (respectful, dependable, supportive, honest, helpful, and so forth). Each of us uses these natural aspirations and expectations to guide us in our interactions. When the I-System captures these aspirations and expectations and makes them requirements, they damage our relationships, closing off our natural executive functioning and affecting our ability to interact appropriately in the relationship.

Let's look at how your natural expectations for yourself can be turned into requirements that weaken your relationships and damage your self-esteem. This exercise focuses on requirements you have for yourself in your relationships with coworkers, in-laws, neighbors, grocery clerks, and so on (for example, *I shouldn't be so angry with my mother-in-law, I should be more assertive with my coworkers, I should be more caring).*

1. My relationship with _____

A. What natural expectations do you have for yourself in this relationship? Example: *I should set better boundaries with my neighbor.*

_____

_____

B. How do you feel and act, and what is your body tension when you don't follow through? Example: *I get angry with myself and my neighbor, I get a stomachache.*

_____

_____

If your answer included body tension and thoughts that you are not good enough or strong enough, your expectation has been turned into a requirement.

C. What are your requirements about this relationship?

_____

_____

D. Use your stress reduction and power building tools to defuse your requirements and change this relationship.

2. List your natural expectations for yourself in other everyday relationships; be as specific as possible. Note if they have been made into requirements.

Natural Expectation	Body Tension If Expectation Is Not Met	Is It Now a Requirement?
I want to get along with my coworker.	*Knot in stomach, shoulders tight*	*Yes*
I will be polite to the grocery clerk.	*None*	*No*

If your requirement isn't met, you're in distress, with your I-System creating the commotion of spinning thoughts and body tension. Look at your requirements and use your stress reduction and power building tools to defuse them. If your natural expectation isn't met, you are naturally disappointed and you handle the situation appropriately with your powerful self.

YOUR MOST IMPORTANT RELATIONSHIP

1. Map your requirements for yourself in your most important relationship. Write the person's name in the oval. Around the oval, scatter your thoughts about how you should be in that relationship (for example, *I shouldn't criticize Jay, I shouldn't upset T. J. when he's tired, I should make Sherri happy*). There's no right or wrong. Be specific and work quickly for the next few minutes.

> ### HOW I SHOULD BE IN MY MOST IMPORTANT
> ### RELATIONSHIP MAP

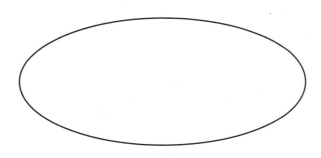

Look at each item and notice any body tension you have when you think about meeting that requirement for how you should be in that relationship. Look again at each item and notice your body tension when you think about *not* meeting that requirement. Thoughts that come with body tension are your requirements.

Is your happiness, love, and commitment based on your I-System's requirements or your natural aspirations and expectations from executive functioning?

_____

_____

2. Do the map again, writing the person's name in the oval. Before you continue writing, listen to background sounds, feel your body's pressure on your seat, sense your feet on the floor, and feel the pen in your hand. Take your time. Once you're settled, keep feeling the pen in your hand, and start writing any thoughts that come to mind about that relationship. As you write, keep paying attention to background sounds, feeling the pen in your hand and watching the ink go onto the paper. Write for a couple of minutes.

HOW I SHOULD BE IN MY MOST IMPORTANT RELATIONSHIP MAP WITH BRIDGING

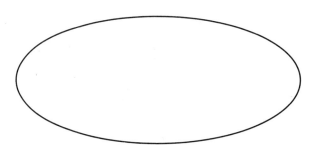

A. In this mind-body state, how do you act?

_____

_____

B. How can this map help you in your relationship?

_____

_____

The release of body tension means you have moved from the I-System loop into the executive functioning loop (see figure 5.1), where you can now function naturally. Although you still have thoughts or natural expectations about how you should be in your relationship, this release of body tension frees you to experience your relationship in a totally different way.

When your overactive I-System switches off, you let go of your requirements and create new opportunities for your most important relationships.

TRANSFORMING YOUR MOST IMPORTANT RELATIONSHIP

You have been building a foundation for your relationship by defusing your requirements for yourself. Now it's time to focus on the requirements you have for your most important other.

1. Do a map of how you think your most important other should act. Write that person's name in the oval. Around the oval, scatter your thoughts for how you want that person to act. Write for a couple of minutes.

> ## HOW MY MOST IMPORTANT OTHER SHOULD ACT MAP

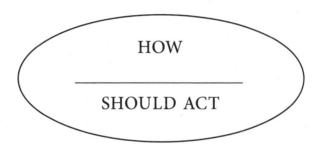

A. Look back over the items on the map and label your requirements with an "R." Next, under each requirement, write what storylines ("SL") you have when the other person does not meet that requirement. Below each thought, note whatever body tension ("BT") you have when the other person doesn't meet your requirement. Take your time doing this map. See the sample map that follows.

B. Are you beginning to see that it's your requirement for how the other person should act that's causing you distress? Yes _____ No _____

C. Now using your bridging awareness practices and thought labeling, go back over your relationship requirements. Take your time. What happens?

_____

When there is a release of body tension, it shows that you are prepared to defuse your requirement when the situation comes up again.

SAMPLE MAP: HOW MY MOST IMPORTANT OTHER SHOULD ACT

(R) He needs to do more around the house
(SL) I do all the work, and I feel angry and taken for granted
(BT) Tight chest

(R) He should take me out to eat more often
(SL) I feel frustrated and ignored
(BT) Headache

(R) She should appreciate me
(SL) Why doesn't she appreciate me?
(BT) Stomachache

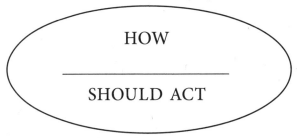

HOW
_____
SHOULD ACT

(R) She should respect how hard I work
(SL) I don't get any slack, I should be able to relax
(BT) Shoulders tight

(R) He should compliment me more
(SL) I feel ignored, he doesn't care
(BT) Tight chest

(R) She should pay attention to me
(SL) I feel angry and unimportant
(BT) Sinking feeling in stomach

R = Requirement

SL = Storyline when requirement is unfulfilled

BT = Body tension when requirement is unfulfilled

2. Write the name of the person from the previous map in the oval below. Next, choose the requirement that still causes you the *most distress* when it's not met (for example, *She should appreciate me*) and write that on the line below. Now scatter your thoughts around the oval for a couple of minutes, describing how things would look if that person *did* meet that requirement. Use as much detail as possible. For example, if the requirement is *She should appreciate me*, you might write, *She would not be critical, She would always have dinner ready, She would say "yes" more,* or *She would be nice to my brother*.

HOW THINGS WOULD LOOK IF MY REQUIREMENT WERE MET MAP

Requirement that causes me the most distress: _____

HOW THINGS
WOULD LOOK IF
_____
MET MY REQUIREMENT

A. Do you really think this will happen? Yes _____ No _____

B. Do you see that an active I-System will continually generate requirements for you and your relationship? Yes _____ No _____

Many people smile when doing this map because they see clearly the nature of their I-System. They see that when requirements are defused, they can handle personal boundaries and basic rights from a position of strength.

WHO'S STILL BUGGING YOU?

Mind-body bridging is not about finding out how you should relate to others; it *is* about finding out how the I-System restricts you and your relationships.

1. Do a requirement map for someone who is still bugging you. In the oval, write the name of the person who continues to trouble you the most. Around the oval, scatter your expectations for how that person should act. Write for a couple of minutes.

> ### TROUBLING PERSON MAP

A. Next, under each item, list any body tension you have when the other person does *not* meet that expectation. Those items are requirements.

B. Describe how the fixer and depressor are dancing in this relationship:

_____

_____

C. What are your storylines?

_____

_____

D. In this mind-body state, how do you act?

_____

2. Do the map again, this time using your bridging awareness practices. Write the same person's name in the oval. Before you continue writing, listen to background sounds, feel your body's pressure on your seat, sense your feet on the floor, and feel the pen in your hand. Take your time. Once you're settled, keep feeling the pen in your hand and start writing any thoughts that come to mind about how that person should act. Watch the ink go onto the paper and keep listening to background sounds. Write for a couple of minutes.

TROUBLING PERSON MAP WITH BRIDGING

MY EXPECTATIONS FOR

_____

A. How do your thoughts on this map (about how that person should act) differ from those on the previous map?

_____

_____

B. What body sensations do you have when you imagine that person not doing what you wrote down on *this* map? The absence of body tension means that the item is not a requirement and that it *is* a natural expectation.

_____

C. In this mind-body state, how do you act?

_____

When your I-System is switched off, your natural aspirations and expectations are just that, and not pressure-driven requirements. Go back to the previous map and use your stress reduction and power building tools on any remaining requirements you had for that person.

When you recognize and defuse requirements you have for both yourself and others, your powerful self, operating in the executive functioning mode with its entire spectrum of experiences, emotions, and gifts, naturally enters into each and every relationship. There is no cookbook for relationships, only the golden key—a resting I-System.

PUTTING IT ALL TOGETHER

A twenty-five-year-old man with a history of being abused as a child would become critical and aloof and "push her away" whenever he and a girlfriend were on the verge of having a close relationship. He finally fell in love. But when they would talk about their future, he would become very anxious and fearful. Even though he knew that these emotions were linked to his abuse and were connected to thoughts of being damaged, unlovable, and bad, he couldn't get past them.

He described his stress reduction and power building tools as his "lifeline to sanity." He began mapping and discovered a requirement that had been causing him distress: *I should be perfect.* Continuing to map about being perfect led to the breakthrough in his relationship. "Perfect" really meant a perfect childhood. The item on the map that changed his life was *I'll always be damaged.* He was able to defuse these requirements about perfection by using his senses; the physical sensations of smelling her perfume, feeling her hand, and experiencing the full-body sensation of a hug served as bridging awareness practices. All aspects of the relationship began improving. He started allowing himself to feel cared for. Three years later he was happily married with a child on the way, and he even had a better job.

Defusing requirements for yourself releases you from the grip of an overactive I-System. You now have access to your powerful self, which participates in your relationships in a healthy way, based on executive functioning.

TOOLS TO DEFUSE REQUIREMENTS FOR YOURSELF

1. Become aware of your earliest signs of an overactive I-System (body tension, depressor thoughts, fixer-driven activities, and storylines about self-criticism), which will prompt you to look for the hidden requirement.

2. Use your bridging awareness practice and thought labeling tools to interrupt the I-System's commotion.

3. Recognize that it's *your* requirement for yourself, not the other person or the situation, causing your distress.

4. You'll know you have defused the requirement when you feel a release of body tension and self-critical mind clutter. When the situation comes up again, your powerful self is in the driver's seat and you are able to deal with it calmly.

As you defuse your requirements for yourself, you create the self-power to defuse the requirements you have in your relationships. When you defuse both sets of requirements (for how you and the other person should be), your powerful self, operating in the executive mode, will keep you out of destructive relationships and optimize the relationships you are in.

Stress Reduction and Power Building Tools

➢ *Defusing requirements for yourself*

➢ *Defusing requirements for your relationships*

MBB EVALUATION SCALE
BUILD A STRESS-FREE FOUNDATION
FOR YOUR RELATIONSHIPS

Date: _____

After using the tools in this chapter for several days, check the description that best matches your practice for each question: hardly ever, occasionally, usually, almost always.

How often do you...	Hardly Ever	Occasionally	Usually	Almost Always
Realize that requirements always activate your I-System, causing stress in your relationships?				
Realize that requirements keep your negative self-image going?				
Improve relationships by defusing requirements?				
See that your requirements for yourself trap you and keep you from being who you really are?				
Experience yourself as far more than who you thought you were?				
Recognize that all you need to do to act from executive functioning is rest your I-System?				
Recognize your powerless self?				
Experience your powerless self as a myth of the I-System?				
Recognize when you are in executive functioning mode?				
Appreciate your powerful self (who you are when you function naturally moment by moment)?				
Appreciate aspects of everyday life in a new light?				
Experience yourself as connected to a wellspring of healing, goodness, and wisdom?				
Notice that your relationships have improved?				
Function better at home and at work?				
Notice an increase in your self-esteem?				

List three requirements for yourself in your relationship that used to cause you stress and that you now deal with by releasing the I-System's tension and letting yourself function in the executive mode:

_____

_____

_____

CHAPTER 7

SUCCESS WITHOUT STRESS

Principle: An overactive I-System restricts your success.

Principle: A resting I-System allows success without stress.

Mind-Body Language:

Mind-body bridging (MBB) action steps: Actions you take to achieve a goal that evolve from mind-body mapping and are carried out by your powerful self, functioning in the executive mode.

YOUR ROAD TO SUCCESS

Success is personal. It's what you want to achieve. Success may include having a loving family, running a 10K, having a satisfying career, holding a high-paying job, having funds to retire, getting an advanced degree, or turning your creative ideas into innovations that benefit you and the world. Success can also be found in finishing a project, taking a great photo, losing five pounds, fixing a special meal, playing a great round of golf, or resolving a sticky situation. When we achieve a particular success, our dualistic mind (chapter 3) may generate thoughts such as *I might lose my great job* or *I could gain back those five pounds*. Those are natural thoughts that will come and go. They will only cause distress if you have the requirement *I shouldn't have negative thoughts*.

The fundamental premise of mind-body bridging is that you have what it takes to live a successful life. The problem arises when your natural thoughts and aspirations about success are captured by your I-System and become requirements (*I should have a great job, I shouldn't gain back those five pounds*). This creates an internal struggle that either prevents success or makes you pay a high price for it. Even if you succeed, the active I-System pushes you on to that next goal before you have a chance to enjoy what you have accomplished.

A health care professional with an anxiety disorder failed her licensing exam. She suffered from vomiting, stomachaches, jitters, and fear of failing whenever she thought about the exam and decided she would never take the exam again. Three years later she was assigned a new supervisor, who was certified in mind-body bridging and began working with her. Soon she discovered that it was not her physical or emotional problems that were holding her back; it was her I-System. A series of mind-body maps led her to uncover one requirement after another. Soon she had a plan, and three months after incorporating mind-body bridging into her life, she retook and passed the exam. Once she was a licensed health care provider, her career blossomed.

This chapter is about removing your I-System's stress-filled obstacles to success. When you defuse your requirements about success, your I-System's roadblocks disappear, allowing your powerful self to flourish.

FEAR PREVENTS SUCCESS

1. Throughout the day, notice the events (for example, *My coworker was fired* or *I'm going to propose*) that led you to become fearful or inhibited. Recognize the underlying requirement (*I shouldn't lose my job, She should say yes*).

Event	Fear	Requirement
Coworker was fired	*I could be fired next.*	*I shouldn't lose my job.*
Marriage proposal	*I'll mess it up, She'll say no*	*She should say yes.*
Bess's party	*I won't fit in, I'll stand out from everyone else*	*I should fit in.*
I recognized a problem and have a solution	*They won't listen and they'll just reject it.*	*They should listen to me and be open to my suggestions.*

2. Think back over the past year and list the three greatest fears that inhibited your success. Find and list the hidden requirements for each:

_____

_____

_____

_____

3. Do a Fear map, writing your greatest fear in the oval. Scatter your thoughts around the oval for a couple of minutes without editing them.

FEAR MAP

A. Note the body tension associated with each item and draw a circle (bubble) around the thought that brings the *most* body tension. Take a few minutes to scatter more thoughts around the circled (bubbled) item. "Bubble" any other troubling items.

B. List your depressor/fixer storylines:

_____

_____

C. Identify and list as many requirements as you can:

_____

_____

_____

Fear is a natural emotion from executive functioning that alerts you to possible danger. It's helpful to consider the fear as having two parts: a thought and a body sensation. When the I-System captures your fears, it convinces you that you can't cope, which can paralyze you, making you a victim of your fear. Fighting the fear never works because your depressor/fixer takes over.

4. Do this map again, writing the same fear in the oval. Before you start writing, listen to background sounds and feel your body's pressure on your seat, your feet on the floor, and the pen in your hand. Take your time. Once you are settled, keep feeling the pen in your hand as you start writing. Watch the ink go onto the paper and listen to background sounds. For the next few minutes, jot down any thoughts that come to mind.

FEAR MAP WITH BRIDGING

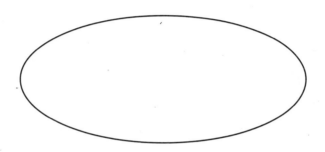

A. What's your mind-body state on this map, compared to the previous one?

_____

_____

B. How would you act differently in this state?

_____

_____

C. Do you think you can defuse your requirements from the previous map the next time the situation comes up? Yes _____ No _____

In mind-body bridging, being fearless doesn't mean you have no fear. Fear is a natural emotion from executive functioning. Being fearless means that your I-System has not paralyzed your natural abilities to deal with the situation that evoked the fear. To control the I-System's influence on your fear, defuse the underlying requirements. When you defuse requirements, rather than react to a fearful situation, you deal with the situation proactively from your powerful self in the executive mode.

OVERTHINKING LIMITS YOU

1.   List five situations where your overthinking bogs you down. Find the requirements behind each event:

Situation	Overthinking	Requirements
Can't sleep the night before making a presentation	*I can't stop going over and over it. I'm making myself anxious and can't get to sleep.*	*I should make a perfect presentation, I should be able to sleep*
Bought an expensive camera to start my own business	*What if I'm no good at it, what if they just laugh at my pictures, Have to have all the equipment I might need*	*I should be creative, I should be successful*
Should I start dating Jack again?	*He seems so right, but he always messes up. He promised to change, but he's said that before.*	*Jack should change for the better, I should make the right decision this time*

The first step in dealing with a situation that is bogging you down is to notice that *overthinking* is a sign of an overactive I-System. Then note other signs of an overactive I-System, like body tension—for example, tight shoulders or a knot in your stomach. Next, use your favorite bridging awareness practice (such as listening to background sounds or rubbing your fingers together) and find your requirement. To defuse a requirement, please remember to recognize that it's not the situation or even your overthinking that is causing your distress; it's your unrecognized requirement. Some requirements are easy to defuse, but if the requirement you are working with is hard to defuse, understand that there may be other, related requirements you haven't found yet. Doing maps like the following ones will help.

2. Map the most troubling situation from the prior list where thinking too much has bogged you down. Write that situation in the oval (for example, *I need to make a decision about this relationship*). Around the oval, scatter your thoughts for a couple of minutes without editing them. Describe your body tension at the bottom of the map.

OVERTHINKING MAP

Body Tension: _____

A. What are your depressor/fixer storylines?

_____

_____

B. Find and list your hidden requirements:

_____

_____

C. If you are still unsettled about anything on your map, "bubble" it by drawing a bubble around the thought that brings the most body tension. Take a few minutes to scatter your thoughts around the bubbled item. Notice your requirements. Bubble any other troubling items.

3. Do the previous map again, writing the same situation in the oval. Before you start writing, listen to background sounds and feel your body's pressure on your seat, your feet on the floor, and the pen in your hand. Take your time. Once you are settled, keep feeling the pen in your hand as you start writing. Watch the ink go onto the paper and listen to background sounds. For the next few minutes, jot down any thoughts that come to mind.

OVERTHINKING MAP WITH BRIDGING

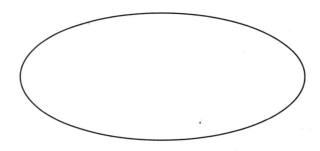

A. What's your mind-body state on this map, compared to the previous map?

_____

_____

B. How would you act differently if you were in this state?

_____

_____

C. Do you see that the real problem is not your thinking, but your I-System being activated by requirements driving your persistent storylines? Yes _____ No _____

D. Describe how you will recognize and defuse your requirements in real time:

_____

_____

EMOTIONS: ASSETS OR LIABILITIES FOR SUCCESS?

1. Do an Emotion map. In the oval, write the emotion that's affecting your success in life the most (for example, *love, joy, happiness, anger, sadness, depression,* or *jealousy*). Around the oval, scatter your thoughts for a couple of minutes without editing them. Describe your body tension at the bottom of the map.

EMOTION MAP

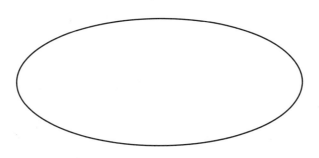

Body Tension: _____

A. Bubble your map, drawing a bubble around a thought that brings lots of body tension. Take a few minutes to scatter more thoughts around the bubbled item. Bubble any other troubling items.

B. Identify and list as many requirements as you can:

_____

_____

_____

C. How do you act in this state?

_____

   When emotions are associated with body tension and mind clutter, they have been captured by the I-System and have become a liability.

2. Do the map again, writing the same emotion in the oval. Before you start writing, listen to background sounds and feel your body's pressure on your seat, your feet on the floor, and the pen in your hand. Take your time. Once you are settled, keep feeling the pen in your hand as you start writing. Watch the ink go onto the paper and listen to background sounds. For the next few minutes, jot down any thoughts that come to mind.

EMOTION MAP WITH BRIDGING

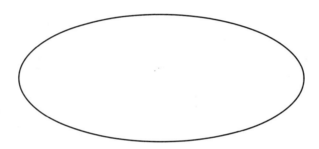

What's your mind-body state after bridging, and how do you act in this state?

_____

_____

The emotions on this map, which are not associated with body tension, are from your powerful self in the executive mode and are all assets.

Emotions, like thoughts, are from executive functioning until the I-System captures them. Every single emotion you will ever experience arises from your reservoir of natural functioning. The I-System captures that emotion and either adds on to it (*so guilty that you can't sleep, can't take care of your responsibilities*) or takes away from it (*so numb to guilt that you continually take advantage of others*).

During the day, when your emotions seem to be getting the best of you, use your bridging awareness practices and thought labeling to recognize the two parts of emotions: *thoughts* and *body sensations*. As you have learned from your bridging map, a calmer mind and body allow you to experience your emotions without the heat of your I-System. This puts your powerful self in the driver's seat. Try it right now. Recall a troubling emotional situation, listen to background sounds, and notice what happens to your body.

WHAT'S STILL HOLDING YOU BACK?

1. Are you still not making the kind of progress you want in your life? List the biggest things holding you back from achieving success. Do they include your looks, brains, ethnic background, kids, lack of money, poor education, trauma, or something else?

_____

_____

2. Do a What's Holding You Back map. In the oval, write the biggest thing that's currently holding you back. Around the oval, scatter your thoughts for a couple of minutes without editing them. Describe your body tension at the bottom of the map.

WHAT'S HOLDING YOU BACK MAP

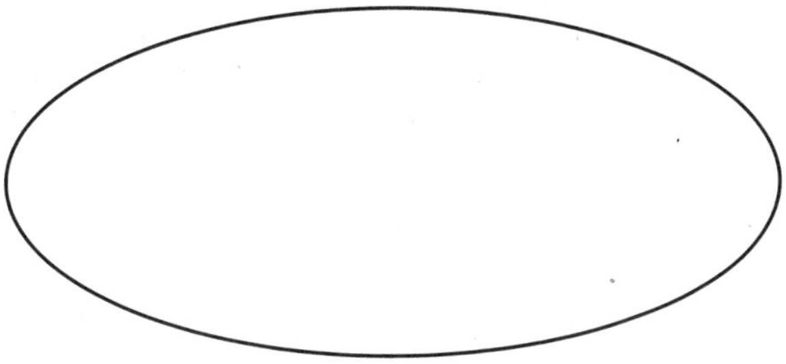

Body Tension: _____

A. List your depressor/fixer storylines:

_____

B. List your requirements:

_____

_____

C. How do you act in this state?

_____

3. Do this map again. In the oval, write the same problem that's holding you back. Before you start writing, listen to background sounds and feel your body's pressure on your seat, your feet on the floor, and the pen in your hand. Take your time. Once you are settled, keep feeling the pen in your hand as you start writing. Watch the ink go onto the paper and listen to background sounds. For the next few minutes, jot down any thoughts that come to mind.

WHAT'S HOLDING YOU BACK MAP WITH BRIDGING

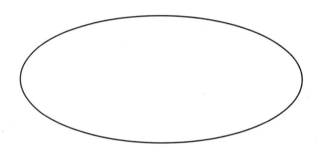

A. What's your mind-body state after bridging?

_____

B. What was really holding you back?

_____

C. Can you see any new opportunities on this map that will let you move forward with your life? List them:

_____

_____

_____

CLARIFYING SUCCESS

Now that you have reduced your I-System's control, let's move on to goals.

1. Scatter around the oval your thoughts about your goals for career, family, or financial success. Write for a couple of minutes without editing your thoughts. Describe your body tension at the bottom of the map.

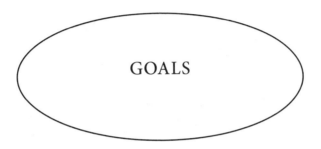

Body Tension: _____

What's your overactive I-System still doing?

A. What are your depressors?

_____

B. What are your fixers?

_____

C. What are your storylines?

_____

D. What are your requirements?

_____

Defusing these requirements is the path to goal fulfillment.

2. Do this map again using bridging awareness practices. Before you start writing, listen to background sounds and feel your body's pressure on your seat, your feet on the floor, and the pen in your hand. Take your time. Once you are settled, keep feeling the pen in your hand as you start writing. Watch the ink go onto the paper and keep listening to background sounds. For the next few minutes, jot down any thoughts that come to mind.

GOALS MAP WITH BRIDGING

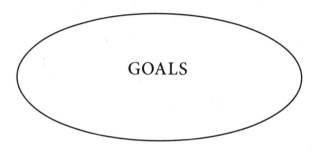

GOALS

A. How is this map the same as or different from the one you just did?

_____

_____

B. Are any of the items on this map associated with body tension? Yes _____ No _____

C. For those items with body tension, do you recognize your requirements? List them:

_____

_____

D. For those items without body tension, are your goals clearer?

_____

_____

DISCOVER MBB ACTION STEPS FOR SUCCESS

Let's put the pedal to the metal and see what action steps are necessary to achieve one of your goals.

1. Select one of the goals from your previous map that was *free* of body tension. Write it in the oval. Next, take a couple of minutes and scatter around the oval your thoughts on what to do to achieve that goal. Be specific. Describe your body tension at the bottom of the map.

ACHIEVING SUCCESS MAP

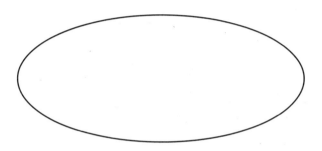

Body Tension: _____

Let's look at what your overactive I-System is doing.

A. What are your depressors?

_____

B. What are your fixers?

_____

C. What are your storylines?

_____

D. What are your requirements?

_____

E. Your requirements are the obstacle that prevents forward motion. Can you defuse them?
   Yes _____ No _____

2. Do this map again using bridging awareness practices. Write the same topic in the oval. Before you start writing down things you can do to achieve your goal, listen to background sounds and feel your body's pressure on your seat, your feet on the floor, and the pen in your hand. Take your time. Once you are settled, keep feeling the pen in your hand as you start writing. Watch the ink go onto the paper and keep listening to background sounds. For the next few minutes, write any thoughts that come to mind.

ACHIEVING SUCCESS MAP WITH BRIDGING

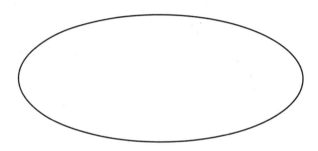

A. Circle those items *without* body tension. These are possible action steps.

B. Choose three of these items as the MBB action steps you want to take to achieve your goal. List them below and begin implementing them in your daily life.

_____

_____

_____

Use this two-part mapping process to separate the I-System's driven steps from the action steps you discover while in the executive mode (bridging awareness map). Remember, the items on your bridging awareness map with *no* associated body tension and mind clutter are all possible MBB action steps. Action steps that are conceived and implemented with an overactive I-System will always limit your outcomes. Use the two-part mapping process every day to navigate through life in the executive mode.

PUTTING IT ALL TOGETHER

This chapter is boot camp for a successful life. By doing the maps at the beginning of the chapter, you slowly removed your self-imposed limitations and stress. This prepares your body and mind for success. Once in shape with a ready and relaxed body and mind, you move forward with ample self-power to clarify your goals. Then you develop MBB action steps that put you on the stress-free road to success. By stress free, we do not mean that your life will be easy. It does not mean that you will not meet with harsh obstacles. It does not mean that your wishes will come true. What it *does* mean is that your I-System (your inner obstacle) will be resting and that each step along your life's path will be directed by your innate wellspring of self-power. You will now face stressors with your powerful self in executive mode.

Annie, a happily married psychologist, had a high-paying federal government job. However, the paperwork and bureaucracy were taking time away from her patients, and her job satisfaction was decreasing. She agonized about this problem for months, and talking with her husband and friends only emphasized that she needed to decide what to do about it. She had a good reputation, so she had many options, including opportunities for advancement within her government agency or a move to the private sector.

Being skilled in mind-body bridging, one night Annie completed the following maps: What's Holding You Back, Clarifying Success, and Action Steps for Success.

Here is what she found.

1. To her great surprise, Annie discovered that she *feared* she wouldn't be successful in another job because her whole career had been with the federal government. She had written *I'm not likable enough and wouldn't succeed at another job* and *I'm fearful of taking risks.*

2. Financial success and job security weren't as important as she thought. What she wanted most of all was to be creative and to help children.

3. Annie's goal of finding a job with the school system was an eye-opener, since most of her experience was with adults.

4. Her MBB action steps were:

   A. Focus my résumé on trauma and its effects on academic performance.

   B. Look for a job opening in the school system.

   C. Begin applying for jobs in the area I want to work in within the next two weeks.

Annie did give up her federal government job and was hired as a school psychologist, developing and implementing programs for high-risk children. She last reported, "I work longer hours than ever, but I have been really creative and feel blessed to experience real success."

Stress Reduction and Power Building Tools

➤ *Defusing requirements to remove self-imposed barriers to success*

➤ *Uncovering and utilizing MBB action steps for success*

MBB EVALUATION SCALE
SUCCESS WITHOUT STRESS

Date: _____

After using the tools in this chapter for several days, check the description that best matches your practice for each question: hardly ever, occasionally, usually, almost always.

How often do you...	Hardly Ever	Occasionally	Usually	Almost Always
Recognize what's holding you back?				
Defuse requirements that hold you back?				
Defuse requirements associated with emotions?				
Defuse requirements about your goals?				
Do two-part MBB Action Steps for Success maps to create action steps?				
Put into place and follow your MBB action steps for success?				
Feel confident about your future?				

List three requirements you have defused:

1. _____

2. _____

3. _____

List three examples of how you have used your stress reduction and power building tools to change your life:

1. _____

2. _____

3. _____

CHAPTER 8

WELLNESS AND SELF-CARE WITHOUT STRESS

Principle: Your undefused requirements restrict who you are and limit your ability to take care of yourself.

Principle: Defusing requirements leads to wellness and a balanced life.

YOUR POWERFUL SELF IN CHARGE

Health-related factors such as poor nutrition, lack of exercise, smoking, excess sun exposure, abuse of alcohol and other substances, inadequate stress management, and disturbances in sleep are increasingly being linked to disease and mortality. Even the latest medical research suggests that over one-third of all cancers are caused by controllable lifestyle factors (Parkin et al. 2011). Most of us attribute our lapses in good self-care to the numerous stressors in our life such as financial constraints, work demands, and family responsibilities; there doesn't seem to be enough time for everything.

By now you know the truth about your I-System. When your overactive I-System is in charge of your lifestyle, your self-care choices become restricted, reducing your quality of life and increasing your chances of illness and early death.

A woman diagnosed with herpes became depressed and withdrawn and didn't follow through with her medical treatment. Feeling hopeless, dirty, worthless, and unlovable, she avoided intimate relationships. After a year of suffering, at the suggestion of her closest friend, she saw a mind-body bridging therapist. Through mapping she recognized that she had been stuck in the dance between her fixer and depressor, and she discovered that her self-loathing was being held in place by requirements she had for herself (*I shouldn't make mistakes, I should be healthy, I should be in control, I should have a perfect body*). As she used her stress reduction and power building tools, she defused her requirements, started feeling better, resumed her medical treatment, and started taking good care of herself.

This chapter puts your powerful self in charge of your self-care and wellness. When your I-System rests, you are in the executive mode, where you naturally achieve wellness, optimize your self-care, and assertively take care of yourself and your responsibilities.

WHO ARE YOU?

Do a Who Am I map. Inside the circle, write the qualities that best describe who you are. After you have listed at least six qualities, outside the circle write the opposite of each quality and connect it with a line. If needed, see the sample map that follows.

WHO AM I MAP

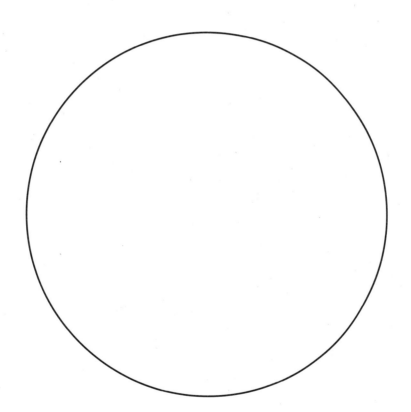

SAMPLE MAP: WHO AM I

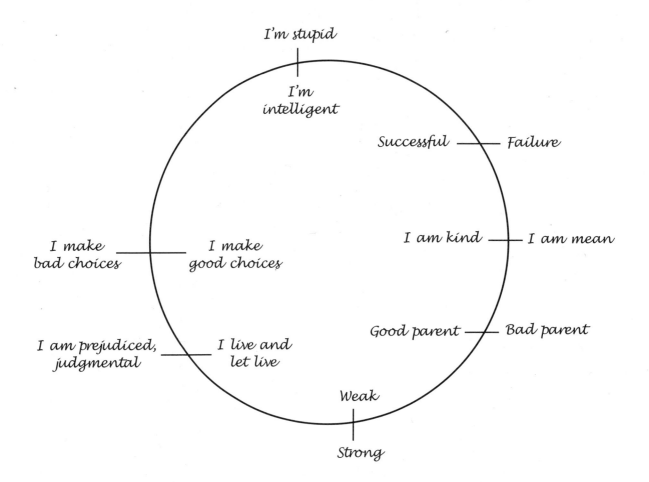

1. How does each quality inside the circle make you feel?

_____

_____

_____

_____

2. How does each quality outside the circle make you feel?

_____

_____

_____

_____

3. Do the qualities inside the circle really describe who you are? Yes _____ No _____

4. Do the qualities outside the circle really describe who you are? Yes _____ No _____

    Your I-System has you believing that the qualities inside the circle define you. Whenever you think you have any of the qualities outside the circle, your I-System tells you you're lacking or damaged. Your I-System wants to convince you that you are who you *think* you are. The qualities you listed are just thoughts about you, not you.

5. Use your bridging awareness practices and thought labeling, and review all the qualities on your map. What happens?

_____

_____

_____

_____

    When you use your bridging awareness practices and thought labeling, you expand the circle to include everything on your map. When you aren't driven by your requirements, you are *everything*, which means you can have any quality on your map (even negative ones) without activating your I-System. When your powerful self is in charge, who you are is no longer a limited picture. Who you are is so vast, boundless, and ever changing that your thinking mind can't grasp it. You are much greater than who you think you are.

WHO'S RUNNING YOUR LIFE—YOU OR YOUR EMOTIONS?

When you are the CEO of your emotions, you bring harmony and balance to your everyday life. You don't need instructions on how to balance love of self with love of others. As long as your I-System is resting, your powerful self is able to deal with the strongest emotions, such as love, happiness, joy, hate, shame, guilt, jealousy, greed, and anger. It's not about the quality or quantity of the emotion you are expressing, it's simply about who's in charge—your constricted, powerless self or your expansive, powerful self. No matter how genuine your love is, or how strong your other emotions are, if your I-System is active, it's going to restrict how you take care of yourself and your relationships.

1. Go back over your past. List three experiences where positive emotions caused you to make poor decisions and not take good care of yourself.

Experience	Positive Emotion
Became so infatuated with my sister's friend that I missed classes and almost flunked out of college	*Love*

2. List three experiences you had where negative emotions caused you to make poor decisions and not take good care of yourself.

Experience	Negative Emotion
Got really mad at my boss, kept it bottled up, and almost had an accident driving home	*Anger*

POSITIVE EMOTIONAL EXPERIENCE

1. From your prior list, select the positive emotion that caused you the most grief and write it in the oval. Take a couple of minutes to write your thoughts around the oval. Work quickly without editing your thoughts.

STRONGEST POSITIVE EMOTION MAP

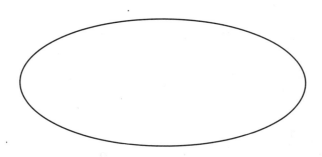

A. Is your mind cluttered or clear?

_____

B. Is your body tense or relaxed? Describe your body tension:

_____

C. Are there depressors or fixers on your map? Yes _____ No _____

D. What are your requirements?

_____

_____

E. How do you take care of yourself in this emotional state?

_____

_____

2. Do this map again. Write the same positive emotion in the oval. Before you continue writing, listen to any background sounds; feel your body's pressure on your seat, sense your feet on the floor, and feel the pen in your hand. Take your time. Once you feel settled, keep feeling the pen in your hand and start writing. Watch the ink go onto the paper, and listen to any background sounds. For the next few minutes, jot down whatever thoughts pop into your mind.

STRONGEST POSITIVE EMOTION MAP WITH BRIDGING

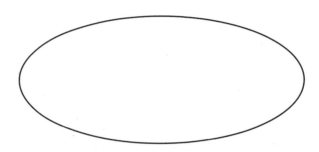

A. What are the differences between the two maps?

_____

_____

B. Is your I-System or your powerful self in charge?

_____

C. Can you defuse the requirements on your previous map? Yes _____ No _____

D. Do you see how your emotions aren't the issue—it's your I-System? Yes _____ No _____

All emotions are from the executive mode. When a situation arises where an emotion is grabbed by the I-System, listen to the background sounds and label your thoughts. It is also helpful to map out your requirements connected to this captured emotion. Resting the I-System always facilitates wellness.

NEGATIVE EMOTIONAL EXPERIENCE

1. From the earlier list, select the negative emotion that caused you the most grief and write it in the oval. Scatter your thoughts around the oval for a couple of minutes.

STRONGEST NEGATIVE EMOTION MAP

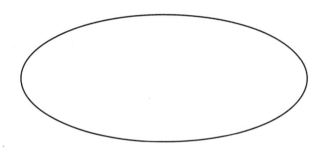

A. Is your mind cluttered or clear?

_____

B. Is your body tense or relaxed? Describe your body tension:

_____

C. Are there depressors or fixers on your map? Yes _____ No _____

D. What are your requirements?

_____

_____

E. How do you take care of yourself in this state?

_____

2. Do this map again. Write the same negative emotion in the oval. Before you continue writing, use your bridging awareness practices. Listen to background sounds and feel your body's pressure on your seat, your feet on the floor, and the pen in your hand. Take your time. Once you are settled, keep feeling the pen in your hand as you start writing. Watch the ink go onto the paper, and listen to background sounds. For the next few minutes, jot down any thoughts that come to mind.

STRONGEST NEGATIVE EMOTION MAP WITH BRIDGING

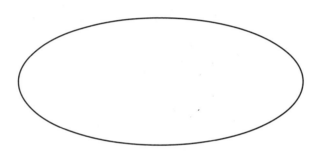

A. What are the differences between the two maps?

_____

_____

B. Is your I-System or your powerful self in charge?

_____

C. Can you defuse the requirements on your previous map? Yes _____ No _____

D. Do you see how your emotions aren't the issue—it's your I-System? Yes _____ No _____

As this map demonstrates, your negative emotions are not your enemy. When you are in the executive mode, your emotions are handled with harmony and balance. Your powerful self functioning in the executive mode automatically orchestrates mind-body wellness.

DO YOUR QUALITIES DEFINE OR CONFINE YOU?

Take a couple of minutes to think about your five most important qualities. Write one of your five most important qualities (for example, *trustworthy, hardworking,* or *loving*) inside each of the sections of the below circle. One or two words will do for each quality. Take a couple of minutes to think about these qualities and then put one quality in each section.

MY FIVE MOST IMPORTANT QUALITIES MAP

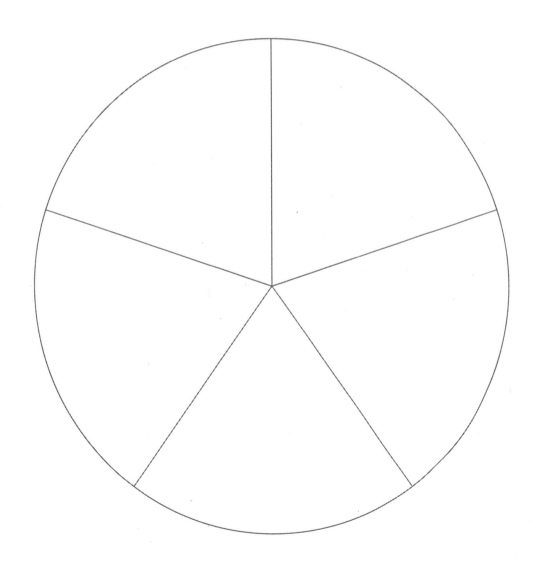

1. Look at your map and cross out the quality that's least important to you. What's your reaction as you imagine yourself without this first quality?

   _____

   _____

   _____

2. Cross out the quality that's the next least important to you. What's your reaction as you imagine yourself without this second quality?

   _____

   _____

   _____

3. Again, cross out the quality that's the next least important to you. What's your reaction as you cross out this third quality?

   _____

   _____

   _____

4. Choose between the last two qualities on your map and cross out the one that's less important to you. What's your reaction when you cross out this next-to-last quality?

   _____

   _____

   _____

5. Think about the last remaining quality. Cross it out. What's your experience now?

   _____

   _____

   _____

The levels of tension and the difficulty in crossing out these naturally functioning qualities shows how strongly the I-System limits you. It captures your qualities and turns them into requirements. It's as if your goodness depends on meeting those requirements. Your reaction when you were crossing out your qualities shows how strongly your I-System tries to define you as a fixed set of qualities. With a calm I-System, your powerful self is no longer limited to a fixed way of seeing yourself.

SELF-CARE GOALS

Now that it's becoming clear who's running your life, let's see who is in charge of your self-care goals.

1. Scatter your thoughts about the most important self-care goals you want to accomplish. Write for a couple of minutes without editing your thoughts. Describe your body tension at the bottom of the map.

SELF-CARE GOALS MAP

Body Tension: _____

As you mull over the map, what's your overactive I-System doing?

A. What are your depressors?

_____

B. What are your fixers?

_____

C. What are your storylines?

_____

D. What are your requirements?

_____

Defusing these requirements is the path to wellness and appropriate self-care.

2. Do this map again using bridging awareness practices. Before you start writing, listen to background sounds and feel your body's pressure on your seat, your feet on the floor, and the pen in your hand. Take your time. Once you are settled, keep feeling the pen in your hand as you start writing. Watch the ink go onto the paper and keep listening to background sounds. For the next few minutes, jot down any thoughts that come to mind.

SELF-CARE GOALS MAP WITH BRIDGING

SELF-CARE GOALS

A. How is this map the same as or different from the previous map?

_____

B. Are any of the items associated with body tension? Yes _____ No _____

C. For those items with body tension, do you recognize your requirements?

_____

_____

D. List the self-care goals that don't have associated body tension:

_____

_____

_____

The solution is not to feel less or more, control less or more; it's simply to quiet your I-System. In this state of wellness you naturally take care of yourself.

DISCOVER MBB ACTION STEPS FOR SELF-CARE

1. Select one of the self-care goals listed on your previous map that was *free* of body tension. Write it in the oval. Next, take a couple of minutes to scatter around the oval your thoughts about what you are going to do to achieve that goal. Be specific. Describe your body tension at the bottom of the map.

SELF-CARE GOAL ACHIEVEMENT MAP

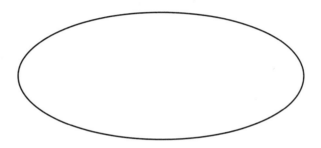

Body Tension: _____

A. What are your depressors?

_____

B. What are your fixers?

_____

C. What are your storylines?

_____

D. What are your requirements?

_____

E. Your requirements are the obstacle that prevents forward motion. Can you defuse them? Yes _____ No _____

   Did you see how your I-System grabbed a goal that was previously without body tension, created requirements about achieving your goal, and restricted your success? Your overactive I-System will always create turmoil and clutter your path to achievement.

2. Do this map again using bridging awareness practices. Write the same topic in the oval. Before you start writing about how you are going to achieve that goal, listen to background sounds and feel your body's pressure on your seat, your feet on the floor, and the pen in your hand. Take your time. Once you are settled, keep feeling the pen in your hand as you start writing. Watch the ink go onto the paper and keep listening to background sounds. Write for a couple of minutes.

SELF-CARE GOAL ACHIEVEMENT MAP WITH BRIDGING

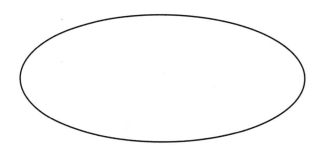

Circle those items *without* body tension. Now, from those items without body tension, choose three MBB action steps you plan to take for stress-free self-care goal achievement.

_____

_____

_____

Remember, action steps that are conceived and implemented with an overactive I-System will always limit your outcome. To be successful, each action step must be carried out with a resting I-System. If any of your action steps are accompanied by body tension and mind clutter, use your stress reduction and power building tools to quiet your I-System. With the I-System no longer in charge of your actions, your choices now come from your executive mode, and the MBB action steps are carried out by your powerful self. You are now heading toward success.

NOW IS THE ONLY TIME YOU CAN TAKE CARE OF YOURSELF

Do a Past, Future, Present map. In the "Past" section of this map, take a couple of minutes to jot down whatever comes to mind about your past. Then describe your body tension. Next, in the "Future" section of this map, take another couple of minutes to write whatever comes to mind about your future. Describe your body tension. Finally, in the "Present" section of this map, take a couple of minutes to jot down whatever comes to mind about the present and, again, describe your body tension.

PAST, FUTURE, AND PRESENT MAP

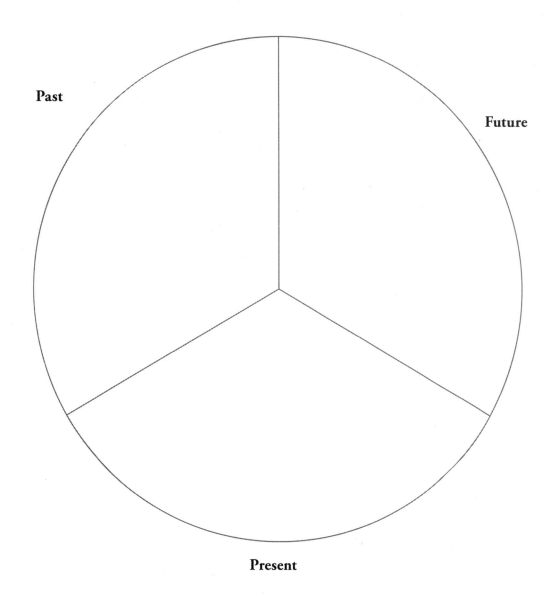

Past

Future

Present

Let's think about this remarkable map:

A. The "Past" section of your map is full of storylines with themes like *My childhood was bad, I made it through by sheer determination,* or *My friends always supported me.* True or not, positive or negative, these stories create mind clutter; they tense your body and take you away from the present. When you recognize storylines in real time, notice that they take you away from doing what you need to do in the present.

What do you notice about the "Past" section of your map? List your storylines:

_____

_____

B. The "Future" section of your map may have a fixer flavor that's full of requirements. Beside each item that brings body tension, write the requirements you can uncover. For instance, if the item creating body tension is *I won't give in to my urges and cravings,* the requirement is *I should not give in to my urges and cravings.* The I-System has captured your naturally functioning thought, turned it into a requirement, and filled your body with tension and your mind with clutter. When thoughts about the future that are driven by the I-System come up in real time, note your body tension, uncover your requirements, and use bridging awareness and thought labeling to bring you back to the present.

List the requirements you notice on the "Future" section of your map:

_____

_____

C. The "Present" section of this map shows what you currently feel and think. Look for signs of an overactive I-System, such as body tension, depressors, fixers, and storylines. Can you uncover your requirements? The I-System has taken stuff from your past and future to try to fix your damaged image of yourself. You now know that the fixer can never "fix" the damage, because you aren't broken. You don't need fixing. The damaged self is caused by your overactive I-System, not what you have been through, and it limits your ability to fully live in the present.

List any signs of an overactive I-System you find in the "Present" section of your map. Also list your depressors, fixers, storylines, and requirements:

_____

_____

_____

_____

_____

3. Do a Present map. Before you start writing about the present, use your bridging awareness practices. Listen to background sounds and feel your body's pressure on your seat, your feet on the floor, and the pen in your hand. Take your time. Once you are settled, keep feeling the pen in your hand as you start writing any thoughts that come to mind about the present. Watch the ink go onto the paper and keep listening to background sounds.

PRESENT MAP WITH BRIDGING

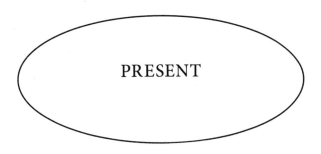

A. What do you notice about this map that's different from the "Present" section of your Past, Future, and Present map?

_____

_____

B. Note how you would live your life in this mind-body state:

_____

_____

Being in the present is not being in a zone, nor is it an enlightenment moment or supernormal state of being. Your powerful self is always available right here, right now. When your I-System is calm, you are in the present. Requirements always take you away from your powerful self living in the present moment. If your depressor has you feeling *not good enough, bored, overwhelmed, lacking,* or *hopeless,* you have a hidden requirement that's pulling you down and taking over your natural executive functioning. On the other hand, when your fixer has you feeling *pushed,* and you feel that *enough is never enough,* you have a hidden requirement that's also taking over your executive functioning. When your I-System is in high gear, look for your hidden requirement and use bridging awareness practices to come back to the present moment and what you were doing.

PUTTING IT ALL TOGETHER

The following account, sent to us from Hong Kong, illustrates a personal journey of revitalization that can be experienced by using the tools in this workbook:

> As an introvert, I tend to feel that I need time on my own to feel good. While I love my friends and enjoy helping people, I've found that socializing wears me out.
>
> Often, after a conversation, fragments of it would echo in my mind, sometimes for hours. Mixed into these fragments were such feelings as regret, indignation, or pride about the way the conversation went or did not go. Perhaps I didn't say all I wanted to, or someone said something I disagreed with, or I made a witty remark. Such thoughts would come and go in my mind as I was doing other things, accompanied by tension in various parts of my body. I often felt wound up and exhausted from this.
>
> I used to try and manage this post-conversation stress by being on my own and waiting for the tension to taper off. Of course, I never knew when it would. With an understanding of bridging, I handle this stress much more easily. The stress can sometimes feel troubling and sometimes be tension-filled euphoria. Either way, I do a What's on My Mind map when I notice the thoughts or body tension. Very quickly, I uncover my requirements, my mind calms down, my body feels at ease, and I feel reenergized.
>
> Some people say an introvert's energy is drained by being around other people. But seeing how quickly I feel reenergized by bridging, I now see it differently for myself. My I-System, when overactive, ties up my energy, and bridging helps to release that energy back into my life.

When your I-System is in control of your self-care, your ability to take care of yourself and meet your responsibilities is restricted and confined. Your choices become limited by the dance of the depressor and fixer and the underlying requirements. How you think, act, and perceive yourself and the world is constricted by the blinders of your I-System. The natural harmony of your mind-body is disrupted, and the stage is set for a variety of health problems.

When your powerful self in the executive mode is in charge of your self-care, your I-System is at rest. With a clearer mind and calmer body, your decisions about your self-care are natural and the choices become clear. A unified mind-body state goes hand in hand with wellness.

Stress Reduction and Power Building Tools

➢ *Defusing requirements to allow appropriate self-care and support wellness*

➢ *Uncovering and utilizing MBB action steps for self-care and wellness*

MBB EVALUATION SCALE
WELLNESS AND SELF-CARE WITHOUT STRESS

Date: _____

After using the tools in this chapter for several days, check the description that best matches your practice for each question: hardly ever, occasionally, usually, almost always.

How often do you...	Hardly Ever	Occasionally	Usually	Almost Always
Recognize when your self-care is driven by your I-System?				
Clearly recognize when you are taking care of yourself naturally with a resting I-System?				
Experience positive emotions with a resting I-System?				
Experience negative emotions with a resting I-System?				
Defuse requirements that interfere with your self-care?				
Experience and express your self-power in the present moment?				
Follow through with self-care MBB action steps?				
Recognize that wellness and a resting I-System go hand in hand?				

List three situations where your I-System interfered with your ability to care for yourself:

1. _____
2. _____
3. _____

List the requirements you were able to defuse that were associated with the situations above:

1. _____
2. _____
3. _____

List three MBB action steps you are taking to ensure wellness:

1. _____
2. _____
3. _____

CHAPTER 9

CRISIS MANAGEMENT

Principle: An unmanaged I-System never stops creating a stress-filled life.

Principle: A resting I-System allows you to confidently and assertively face any challenge with your powerful self, functioning in the executive mode.

FACING CHALLENGES

The future is often uncertain and unpredictable. We don't have control over what the future has in store for us. What you do have control over is who is in charge, your I-System or your powerful self. When the I-System is in the driver's seat, challenges become crises as you are filled with stress and feel powerless. By integrating your stress reduction and power building tools into your everyday life even when you face a full-blown crisis, you have the ability to do so in the executive mode with your powerful self making the best choices.

A thirty-year-old man's wife of four months was leaving him for another man. He persuaded her to go away with him to a small cottage in the forest, near a beautiful river, for a "last chance weekend." He planned to make this a very romantic time and to persuade her to stay with him. When mapping, he realized how tense and anxious he was about the "perfect walk in the woods" where he planned to state his case. Recognizing his fixer activity and requirements, he rested his I-System. The day of the planned walk, his wife slept till noon. Instead of demanding she get up so they could follow the schedule he'd made, he built a fire in the fireplace and sat watching the flames and listening to the crackling sounds of the logs. "Thanks to the maps I did before the trip, I knew that what I wanted to happen during the walk was just a bunch of my requirements," he said. "I waited for her to quietly wake up and then we had a wonderful time together."

Here's how others have used mind-body bridging for crisis management:

A young woman with a history of substance abuse had been using mind-body bridging for three months. Her brother died suddenly from a heart attack and then another close relative died in an auto accident. Using her stress reduction and power building tools, she mapped about her brother's death, uncovering requirements like *My brother shouldn't have died* and storylines like *Why him? He was so good.* and *I was the bad one.* Her bridging map calmed her I-System and gave her access to her wellspring of power. Feeling at peace with herself, she didn't relapse, and she became a support for other family members.

A fifty-five-year-old woman facing a quadruple bypass was able to get through her recovery with excellent results and without pain meds using her strong mind-body bridging practices. "Mind-body bridging kept my mind-body-spirit working on the same page during recovery."

A forty-year-old businessman with a $246,000 IRS bill felt helpless, ruminated over his financial situation, and had unremitting headaches. After several weeks of mind-body bridging, his headaches disappeared, he was able to sleep and work, and his family relationships returned to normal. Six months later, he continues to work with the IRS and his tax attorney without a recurrence of his symptoms.

A liver cancer patient with insomnia, night sweats, and anxiety used mind-body bridging to sleep through the night and awaken refreshed. Mapping reduced her anxiety, and listening to the background sounds helped her sleep.

A seventy-year-old man with chronic pulmonary disease was on oxygen most of the day. He began feeling fearful and anxious about not having enough oxygen when he left his home. Becoming depressed, he curtailed his activities. After he learned mind-body bridging, his awareness of sensations other than his breathing helped him relax and reduced his respiratory rate. He defused his requirement about not having enough oxygen, began planning for excursions, and two years later is living an active life.

The parents of Oliver, a child with autism spectrum disorder, were at their wits' end. They both needed to maintain an active social life for professional reasons. By the time Oliver reached five he would gravitate to their guests and start sucking on bits of their clothes. After learning mind-body bridging his parents recognized their requirements and began mapping them out. They were able to switch off their

I-System and discover MBB action steps. "We had the know-how before; it's amazing how our I-Systems prevented us from being relaxed and creative with Oliver."

A man with terminal cancer used his senses every day, defused his requirements about his restrictive lifestyle, and was able to dramatically improve the quality of his life. "Knowing I have terminal cancer, I appreciate every sight, sound, and sensation. It's like my senses keep me alive. Life is good."

By mapping various situations that often lead to a crisis, this chapter brings together all your stress reduction and power building tools so you can effectively handle whatever challenges come up in life.

TIME MANAGEMENT

Facing a situation where you don't have enough time can really generate stress.

1. Throughout the day pay attention to how you experience time. Do you have enough of it? Do you want more? Does it pass you by? How do you use it? Does it create stress?

2. Do a Time map. Write in the oval a situation that created stress because you didn't have enough time to complete the task. Write for a couple of minutes.

```
         ╭─────────────────────────╮
        ╱                           ╲
       │      I DIDN'T HAVE          │
       │    ENOUGH TIME TO           │
       │                             │
       │   _____       │
        ╲                           ╱
         ╰─────────────────────────╯
```

A. Is your mind cluttered or clear?

_____

B. Is your body tense or relaxed? List your body sensations:

_____

C. What are your storylines?

_____

_____

D. What are your requirements?

_____

_____

E. How do you act in this mind-body state?

_____

3. Do this map again using bridging awareness practices. Write the same situation in the oval. Before you continue writing, listen to background sounds and feel your body's pressure on your seat, your feet on the floor, and the pen in your hand. Take your time. Once you are settled, keep feeling the pen in your hand as you start writing. Watch the ink go onto the paper and keep listening to background sounds. For the next few minutes, jot down any thoughts that come to mind.

TIME MAP WITH BRIDGING

I DIDN'T HAVE
ENOUGH TIME TO

_____

A. How is this map different from the previous map?

_____

B. Is it time or your requirements that generate your stress?

_____

_____

C. How do you act in this mind-body state?

_____

When you compare your time maps, you will see how your I-System interferes with completing your tasks.

MIND-BODY WORKBOOK FOR STRESS

HANDLING DIFFICULT CHOICES AND THEIR CONSEQUENCES

1. Do a Choices and Their Consequences map. Scatter around the oval the choices you might be facing in the near future that could impact your life (for example, *changing jobs, having a baby, starting a new business, relocating to a new city, having that honest talk, missing our son's game again, getting a divorce*). Write for a couple of minutes. Next, write some possible consequences under each item.

CHOICES AND
THEIR CONSEQUENCES

A. Is your mind cluttered or clear?

_____

B. Is your body tense or relaxed? What are your body sensations?

_____

C. What were your fixers?

_____

D. What were your storylines?

_____

E. List your requirements:

_____

F. How do you act in this mind-body state?

_____

170

2. Do this map again using bridging awareness practices. Before you start writing, listen to background sounds and feel your body's pressure on your seat, your feet on the floor, and the pen in your hand. Take your time. Once you are settled, keep feeling the pen in your hand as you start writing. Watch the ink go onto the paper and keep listening to background sounds. For the next few minutes, jot down any thoughts that come to mind about your choices and their consequences.

CHOICES AND THEIR CONSEQUENCES MAP WITH BRIDGING

```
              CHOICES AND
          THEIR CONSEQUENCES
```

A. What do you notice that is different on this map?

_____

B. How do you act with a resting I-System?

_____

C. How will you defuse your requirements on the previous map when they come up during your day?

_____

Using this two-part map not only reduces your stress, it improves your decision making and avoids future problems.

WORST POSSIBLE THING

1. Take a few moments to consider the worst possible thing that can happen to you and write it in the oval. Now do a Worst Possible Thing That Can Happen to Me map. Scatter your thoughts around the oval for a couple of minutes. Describe your body tension at the bottom of the map.

THE WORST
POSSIBLE THING THAT
CAN HAPPEN TO ME IS
_____

Body Tension: _____

A. Looking at your map, list any signs of your overactive I-System:

_____

_____

B. List the requirements you find:

_____

_____

_____

C. To uncover more requirements, do a bubble map for any troubling thoughts that are causing body tension.

2. Do this map again, writing the same thing in the oval. Before you start writing, use your bridging awareness practices. Listen to background sounds and feel your body's pressure on your seat, your feet on the floor, and the pen in your hand. Take your time. Once you are settled, keep feeling the pen in your hand as you start writing. Watch the ink go onto the paper and listen to background sounds. For the next few minutes, jot down any thoughts that come to mind about the worst possible thing that can happen to you.

> ## THE WORST POSSIBLE THING THAT CAN HAPPEN TO ME MAP WITH BRIDGING

THE WORST POSSIBLE THING THAT CAN HAPPEN TO ME IS

_____

A. What do you notice that's different on this map?

_____

_____

B. How do you act with a calm I-System?

_____

_____

C. How will you defuse the requirements on your previous map when they come up during your day?

_____

_____

D. Does the situation in the oval disconnect you from your powerful self? Yes _____ No _____

E. Is it clear that your powerful self is always within you, no matter what? Yes _____ No _____

CRISIS MANAGEMENT

1. Whenever and wherever you face a crisis, it's helpful to do a Crisis map. For this exercise, choose a crisis, big or small, in your life. Write the crisis in the oval. Take a couple of minutes to write around the oval whatever pops into your mind about how you can handle the crisis. Work quickly, without editing your thoughts. Your mind produces hundreds of thoughts each minute; the more open you are, the more insight you gain.

MY CRISIS IS

_____

A. Is your mind cluttered or clear?

_____

B. Describe your body tension:

_____

C. What are your requirements?

_____

_____

D. How would you act in this mind-body state?

_____

2. Do this map using your bridging awareness practices. Write the same crisis in the oval. Before you start writing about how you can handle the crisis, listen to any background sounds; feel your body's pressure on your seat, sense your feet on the floor, and feel the pen in your hand. Take your time. Once you feel settled, keep feeling the pen in your hand and start writing. Watch the ink go onto the paper, and listen to any background sounds. For the next few minutes, write down whatever thoughts pop into your mind about your crisis.

CRISIS MAP WITH BRIDGING

MY CRISIS IS

_____

Observe the differences between the two maps:

A. From the items on your map without body tension, list three MBB action steps:

_____

_____

_____

B. Are you now better equipped to deal with the crisis? Yes _____ No _____

Doing these maps takes less than five minutes and helps you avoid many of the pitfalls of the past.

USING YOUR STRESS REDUCTION AND POWER BUILDING TOOLS TO MANAGE CRISES

1. When you are faced with a crisis and you have the signs of an active I-System, use your bridging awareness practices, thought labeling, and depressor/fixer recognition and uncover and defuse your requirements.

2. Take a few minutes to complete a two-part Crisis Management map. Be open to the executive functioning choices that present themselves.

3. Live a full life with a resting I-System.

PUTTING IT ALL TOGETHER

You have used your stress reduction and power building tools, have mapped, recognized, and defused your requirements, and have developed MBB action steps to deal with a crisis. You now know how to deal with any crisis with a resting I-System. Remember, each moment your I-System is in control is a crisis because it's a moment filled with stress and powerlessness. When your powerful self in the executive mode is handling a crisis, the decisions you make guide you to your better life.

Stress Reduction and Power Building Tools

➢ *Uncovering and utilizing MBB action steps for crisis management*

➢ *Living life with a resting I-System*

MBB EVALUATION SCALE
CRISIS MANAGEMENT

Date: _____

After using the tools in this chapter for several days, check the description that best matches your practice for each question: hardly ever, occasionally, usually, almost always.

How often do you...	Hardly Ever	Occasionally	Usually	Almost Always
Listen to background sounds?				
Sense the sensation under your fingers when you take a drink?				
Experience gravity?				
Use bridging practices to bust stress or melt misery?				
Become keenly aware of everyday activities such as making the bed, eating, and driving?				
Hear the water going down the drain and experience the water on your body when showering or washing your hands?				
Use bridging to help you sleep?				
Use bridging to help you relax and stay focused?				
Use body sensations as a sign of an overactive I-System?				
Recognize an overactive I-System is underlying your problem?				
Recognize and defuse your depressor?				
Recognize and defuse your fixer?				
Recognize and defuse requirements that are causing your daily upsets?				
Recognize and defuse storylines?				
Recognize and experience that the powerless self is a myth of the I-System?				
Appreciate your powerful self naturally functioning moment by moment?				
Make daily mind-body maps?				
Use MBB action steps?				
Use your crisis management tools?				
Live life in the executive mode with your powerful self in charge?				

MBB SELF-POWER INDICATOR

Date: _____

This indicator should be completed only when you have integrated the stress reduction and power building tools from this workbook into your life. Please compare your scores with those for the self-power indicators in chapters 1 and 4. This indicator lets you objectively note your progress and systematically keep track of your life-changing experiences.

Over the past seven days, how did you do in these areas?

Circle the number under your answer.	**Not at all**	**Several days**	**More than half the days**	**Nearly every day**
1. I've had positive interest and pleasure in my activities.	0	1	3	5
2. I've felt optimistic, excited, and hopeful.	0	1	3	5
3. I've slept well and woken up feeling refreshed.	0	1	3	5
4. I've had lots of energy.	0	1	3	5
5. I've been able to focus on tasks and use self-discipline.	0	1	3	5
6. I've stayed healthy, eaten well, exercised, and had fun.	0	1	3	5
7. I've felt good about my relationships with my family and friends.	0	1	3	5
8. I've been satisfied with my accomplishments at home, work, or school.	0	1	3	5
9. I've been comfortable with my financial situation.	0	1	3	5
10. I've felt good about the spiritual base of my life.	0	1	3	5
11. I've been satisfied with the direction of my life.	0	1	3	5
12. I've felt fulfilled, with a sense of well-being and peace of mind.	0	1	3	5

Score Key: Column Total   ____   ____   ____   ____

0-15 . . . . .Poor Self-Power

16-30 . . . . Fair Self-Power   Total Score _____

31-45 . . . . .Good Self-Power

46 and above . . . . Excellent Self-Power

CONCLUSION

The design of this book is based on over a decade of research and clinical experience and is individually adapted for you as you complete the exercises. Each mind-body bridging map is uniquely you. The appendices contain a two-part mapping template you can use for your daily ongoing mapping practice. Remember, when you use your stress reduction and power building tools, your inner power, wisdom, and beauty flow into your everyday life.

Stress Reduction and Power Building Tools

CHAPTER 1

> ➢ *Recognizing when your I-System is active or inactive*

> ➢ *Thought labeling*

> ➢ *Bridging awareness practices*

>> • *Awareness of background sounds*

>> • *Awareness of what you are touching*

>> • *Awareness of colors, facial features, shapes*

>> • *Awareness of your body sensations*

CHAPTER 2

> ➢ *Using your body as a compass*

> ➢ *Creating two-part mind-body bridging maps*

> ➢ *Discovering requirements that activate your I-System*

> ➢ *Using requirement recognition to quiet your I-System*

CHAPTER 3

> ➢ *Recognizing the depressor's activity*

> ➢ *Storyline awareness*

> ➢ *Defusing the depressor*

CHAPTER 4

> *Defusing the fixer*

> *Recognizing the depressor/fixer cycle*

> *Converting fixer activity into executive functioning*

CHAPTER 5

> *Defusing requirements for others and for situations*

CHAPTER 6

> *Defusing requirements for yourself*

> *Defusing requirements for your relationships*

CHAPTER 7

> *Defusing requirements to remove self-imposed barriers to success*

> *Uncovering and utilizing MBB action steps for success*

CHAPTER 8

> *Defusing requirements to allow appropriate self-care and support wellness*

> *Uncovering and utilizing MBB action steps for self-care and wellness*

CHAPTER 9

> *Uncovering and using MBB action steps for crisis management*

> *Living life with a resting I-System*

Congratulations on completing this workbook! You have gained a unique freedom—the ability to live your life in the executive functioning mode with a resting I-System. With the stress reduction and power building tools you have learned in this workbook, you can now live your best life with your powerful self in charge.

APPENDIX: DAILY MAPPING GUIDE FOR MIND-BODY BRIDGING

1. Choose a mapping topic and write it in the oval. It may be a general question like "What's on My Mind?" or a specific question about a troubling situation. Next, take a couple of minutes to scatter around the oval your thoughts about that topic. Be specific. Describe your body tension at the bottom of the map.

CHOOSE YOUR TOPIC MAP

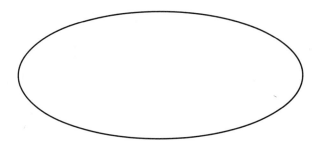

Body Tension: _____

Look at what your overactive I-System is doing.

A. What are your depressors?

_____

B. What are your fixers?

_____

C. What are your storylines?

_____

D. What are your requirements?

_____

E. How do you act in this mind-body state?

_____

2. Do this map again using bridging awareness practices. Write the same topic in the oval. Before you start writing about the topic, listen to background sounds and feel your body's pressure on your seat, your feet on the floor, and the pen in your hand. Take your time. Once you are settled, keep feeling the pen in your hand as you start writing. Watch the ink go onto the paper, and keep listening to background sounds. Write for a couple of minutes.

CHOOSE YOUR TOPIC MAP WITH BRIDGING

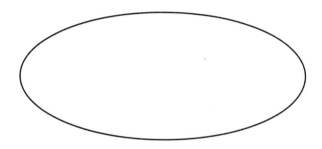

A. How is this map the same as or different from the previous one?

_____

_____

B. How do you act in this mind-body state?

_____

_____

C. Are you able to defuse the requirement on the previous map?

_____

_____

The insights gained through this two-part map can now be used in your life.

APPENDIX: MIND-BODY LANGUAGE

CHAPTER 1:

I-System: Everyone has an I-System, and it's either active or resting. You know the I-System is active when your mind is cluttered with spinning thoughts, your body is tense, your awareness contracts, and your mental and physical functioning is impaired. It's called the I-System because it prompts you to falsely identify with the spinning thoughts and the physical distress it causes.

Powerful self: How you think, feel, see the world, and act when your I-System is resting. Your mind and body operate harmoniously as a unit and stressors are handled smoothly and efficiently.

Mind-body bridging: When you use the stress reduction and power building tools in this workbook, the mind and body are unified. A bridge is formed from a stressful state with an overactive I-System to a powerful self functioning in the executive mode.

CHAPTER 2:

Requirements: Mental rules your I-System has created for you about how you and the world should be at any moment. Your I-System is activated when these rules are broken.

Requirement recognition: When you become clearly aware that it is *your requirement*, and not the stressor, activating your I-System, you reduce stress and gain self-power.

CHAPTER 3:

Powerless self: How you think, feel, and act when your I-System is overactive. Life is overwhelming, your executive functioning is impaired, and you struggle vainly to keep it all together.

Depressor: A part of the I-System that captures your natural negative thoughts and self-talk and creates body tension and mind clutter.

Storyline: Thoughts spun into stories by your I-System that pull you away from what you are presently doing.

Defusing the depressor: When you become clearly aware (in real time) that your negative thoughts are "just thoughts," those thoughts are then prevented from creating body tension and mind clutter.

CHAPTER 4:

Fixer: The depressor's partner that drives you with overactive, never-ending thoughts of how to fix yourself and the world.

Defusing the fixer: When you become clearly aware (during an activity) that your fixer is active and use your stress reduction and power building tools, you take away the fixer's power. You immediately experience a shift from a stressful driven state to one with a ready and relaxed mind and body. You now actively and assertively take care of yourself and your responsibilities in the executive functioning mode.

Depressor/fixer cycle: These I-System partners create a vicious cycle, stop you from reaching your goals, and keep the I-System going and going.

CHAPTER 5:

Defusing requirements: When using all your stress reduction and power building tools, you handle a situation that previously activated your I-System with a stress-free, ready, and relaxed mind and body. Even when the picture of how you and the world should be is not fulfilled, the requirement is powerless to activate your I-System.

CHAPTER 7:

Mind-body bridging (MBB) action steps: Actions you take to achieve a goal that evolve from mind-body mapping and are carried out by your powerful self, functioning in the executive mode.

REFERENCES

Ansell, E. B., K. Rando, K. Tuit, J. Guarnacci, and R. Sinha. 2012. "Cumulative Adversity and Smaller Gray Matter Volume in Medial Prefrontal, Anterior Cingulate, and Insula Regions." *Biological Psychiatry* 72(1): 57–64.

Block, S. H., and C. B. Block. 2007. *Come to Your Senses: Demystifying the Mind-Body Connection.* 2nd ed. New York: Atria Books/Beyond Words Publishing.

———. 2010. *Mind-Body Workbook for PTSD: A 10-Week Program for Healing After Trauma.* Oakland, CA: New Harbinger Publications.

Block, S. H., S. H. Ho, and Y. Nakamura. 2009. "A Brain Basis for Transforming Consciousness with Mind-Body Bridging." Paper presented at Toward a Science of Consciousness conference, June 12, at Hong Kong Polytechnical University, Hong Kong, China, Abstract 93.

Boly, M., C. Phillips, E. Balreau, C. Schnakers, C. Degueldre, G. Moonen, et al. 2008. "Consciousness and Cerebral Baseline Activity Fluctuations." *Human Brain Mapping* 29 (7): 868–74.

Boly, M., C. Phillips, L. Tshibanda, A. Vanhaudenhuyse, M. Schabus, T. T. Dang-Vu, et al. 2008. "Intrinsic Brain Activity in Altered States of Consciousness: How Conscious Is the Default Mode of Brain Function?" *Annals of the New York Academy of Sciences* 1129: 119–29.

Lipschitz, D. L., R. Kuhn, A. Y. Kinney, G. W. Donaldson, and Y. Nakamura. 2012. "Reduction in Salivary Alpha-amylase Levels Following Mind-Body Interventions in Cancer Survivors." Under review.

Nakamura, Y., D. L. Lipschitz, R. Kuhn, A. Y. Kinney, and G. W. Donaldson. Forthcoming. "Investigating Efficacy of Two Mind-Body Intervention Programs for Managing Sleep Disturbance in Cancer Survivors: A Randomized Controlled Trial." *Journal of Cancer Survivorship.*

Nakamura, Y., D. L. Lipschitz, R. Landward, R. Kuhn, and G. West. 2011. "Two Sessions of Sleep-Focused Mind-Body Bridging Improve Self-Reported Symptoms of Sleep and PTSD in Veterans: A Pilot Randomized Controlled Trial." *Journal of Psychosomatic Research* 70 (4): 335–45.

Parkin, M., L. Boyd, S. Darby, D. Mesher, P. Sasiene, L. Walker, et al. 2011. "The Fraction of Cancer Attributable to Lifestyle and Environmental Factors in the UK in 2010." *British Journal of Cancer* 105: S2 (Si–S81).

Tollefson, D. R., K. Webb, D. Shumway, S. H. Block, and Y. Nakamura. 2009. "A Mind-Body Approach to Domestic Violence Perpetrator Treatment: Program Overview and Preliminary Outcomes." *Journal of Aggression, Maltreatment, and Trauma* 18 (1): 17–45.

Weissman, D. H., K. C. Roberts, K. M. Visscher, and M. G. Woldorff. 2006. "The Neural Bases of Momentary Lapses in Attention." *Nature Neuroscience* 9 (7): 971–78.

Stanley H. Block, MD, is adjunct professor of psychiatry at the University of Utah School of Medicine, and a board-certified psychiatrist and psychoanalyst. He is a consultant on the medical staff at U.S. Army and Veterans Administration Hospitals. He lectures and consults with treatment centers worldwide and is coauthor of *Mind-Body Workbook for PTSD* and *Come to Your Senses*. He and his wife, Carolyn Bryant Block, live in Copalis Beach, WA. Find out more about his work online at sleepstar.co and mindbody bridging.com.

Carolyn Bryant Block is coauthor of *Bridging the I-System*, *Come to Your Senses*, and *Mind-Body Workbook for PTSD*. She is also the co-developer of mind-body bridging and identity system (I-System) theory and techniques.

Andrea A. Peters is an educator certified in mind-body bridging. She guided the organizational development of mind-body bridging material.